GEOGRAPHY BEE DECLASSIFIED – U.S. FILES

GEOGRAPHY BEE DECLASSIFIED – U.S. FILES

(Revised)

Ram Iyer

Edited by
GENTRY CLARK

ISBN: 1508569215
ISBN 13: 9781508569213

CONTENTS

ACKNOWLEDGMENTS

I would like to thank my family, friends, past and current participants, and their parents for having played a major part in motivating me to write this study guide. I would also like to thank Gentry Clark who helped me edit this guide and provide valuable input and suggestions when needed. I take pride in the fact that this guide received generous help from many competitors from the past and the present who have helped enhance the quality of the guide.

INTRODUCTION

Why this guide?

After the successful launch of my two guides *Geography Bee Simplified* and *Geography Bee Demystified*, I realized that there is a need for a guide devoted exclusively to U.S. geography. ***Geography Bee Declassified – U.S. Files* is the result**. This guide is targeted towards preparing for the School and State Geography Bees. Many readers appreciated the fact that my previous guides do not elaborate upon the various steps involved in the bee. Rules of the competition and information about registration and preparation are explained on the National Geographic Society's website. Instead, this guide gives advice about how to perform in the competitions and gets to the meat of the competition, the questions, right away.

Who is this guide for?

This guide is for serious contestants. It is for those who already have mastered the basic facts about United States and who have a good shot at advancing to the higher levels at their school and state competitions.

How is the guide organized?

Geography Bee Declassified – U.S. Files is divided into seven chapters based on the different regions in United States. The last chapter acts as a catch-all for questions that were not found in other chapters. The question-and-answer format lends itself to an easier way of studying for those who have limited time to prepare for the Geography Bee.

How do I use this guide?

This guide is most useful with the companionship of a good atlas, such as those published by the National Geographic Society. You can see the Bibliography to get more details. Don't forget to look at the wealth of information available at www.nationalgeographic.com/geobee

Take the daily GeoBee Challenge from the National Geographic website every day and make a note of all the questions that are difficult. The resources are free and are informative. Use this guide in conjunction with these resources. To do well, you may need to use multiple resources.

Some helpful hints...

The Geography Bee competition format is not set in stone. In fact, changes in format do happen without advance notice. However, based on my close personal experience with previous competitions, I would like to address some of the questions that readers may have and offer some helpful hints.

Are questions in this guide compiled from various competitions conducted by the National Geographic Society?

The answer is "no." Although the guide is written to help prepare for the competitions, using the exact questions from the competitions not only is unethical but would also defeat the very purpose behind the National Geographic Society's competitions. The goal of the National Geographic Society is to increase geography awareness around the country. The competition does not lend itself to a "cramming" session. Instead, it seeks to develop an appreciation of geography. If you have had some experience listening to many of the questions asked, you will realize that the wealth of information delivered through these questions is probably more educational than the question being asked. For example, you will rarely find a question that merely asks, "What is the capital of Georgia?"

Instead, what you will hear is information about Atlanta delivered in the question in the competition. In keeping with that spirit, I have done my best to avoid questions that resemble what I have already seen or heard. If there are similarities to some of the questions from past competitions, it is purely a coincidence.

How do I prepare? I have other classes, I have a busy schedule at school, and my parents work late.

This is a fact of life. In fact, for most students, mid-term exams may coincide with the School Bee. The earlier you prepare the better. This guide has been written with a view to give participants, under these conditions, some help in developing a game plan. It is not a bad idea to have a simple atlas and a globe at home and find time to spend 15 minutes or 30 minutes a day on preparation for the Geography Bee. A few extra hours during the weekend also helps. You can start by referring to children's atlases that are available on the market several months before the competitions start. The local library is a great resource. In addition, use this guide to supplement your knowledge and to develop a knack for answering questions and filtering out data from questions that may appear confusing. It is not uncommon to find extraneous data added to a question that could be distracting. If you learn how to focus on the clues and get to the real question, you are halfway there.

To get the best out of this guide, you have to be ready with your atlas and physically locate the answer to each question on the map, and then try to read more about it. As you locate a place, try to see what is around that location. Often times, questions in these competitions tend to use the surrounding places or physical terrain in the adjacent areas as hints. Very seldom will you find a question stated exactly as what you find in the books you have. In other words, you have to know your geography, not just the answers. It is not, however, too complex. The National Geographic Society competitions do not test contestants on trivia. They are about places you often hear but did not realize their importance. There are no trick questions.

What did the pronouncer say?

During the competition, what should you do if you are not sure what you heard? Use your quota of repeats. Do not, however, waste your repository of repeats by asking the announcer merely to repeat the question. Often, you did hear the question right the first time! Instead, ask the pronouncer to spell it. You may be surprised to find that you had known the answer all along.

Use your allotted time.

You have 15 seconds to answer a question. Use it. Do not answer a question immediately after it is read—wait until you are in the seventh second. The same concept applies to the State Bee qualifying test. If you finish the written test early, read your answers again. In populous states like California and New York, this could be critical. There are no bonus points for finishing early.

Disclaimer

The information provided in this guide is based on my own research and that of several geography enthusiasts. Despite input from several knowledgeable individuals, the guide is not guaranteed to be without inaccuracies. Answers may be subject to interpretation and/or reliable sources could offer different data. If there are inconsistencies between sources, readers should follow National Geographic standards and their resources. As you use this guide if you find any errors, please bring them to my attention so that future editions and subsequent versions can be improved. (Please state your sources when you send a correction.)

Please visit http://www.geographybee-coaching.com/ to send your suggestions or corrections. This site may also have new announcements, updates, corrections, and new quizzes.

CHAPTER 1

U.S. Northeast

1. The city of Bellefonte is located in the Allegheny region of what U.S. state?
    Pennsylvania

2. What U.S. state borders New Brunswick, Canada?
    Maine

3. What northeastern U.S. state borders only one of the great lakes, Lake Erie?
    Pennsylvania

4. What state borders Delaware, Pennsylvania, and West Virginia?
    Maryland

5. The Genesee River rises in what plateau?
    Appalachian Plateau

6. What river rises in Otsego Lake in Central New York?
    Susquehanna River

7. The North Branch River forms a border between West Virginia and what state?
    Maryland

8. What state borders both Vermont and New Hampshire to their south?
    Massachusetts

9. Which state does not border Connecticut – New Jersey, Rhode Island, or New York?
    New Jersey

10. Which state extends farther north – New Jersey or Pennsylvania?
    Pennsylvania

11. The easternmost point of Lake Erie is in what state?
New York

12. Which state has a shorter coastline – New Hampshire or Rhode Island?
New Hampshire

13. A city in Pennsylvania's Lehigh Valley was named on Christmas Eve in 1741 by Count Zinzendorf of Saxony. Name this city originally settled by the Moravians, the oldest Protestant denomination in the world.
Bethlehem

14. The city of Mount Vernon is a suburb of what large city in the U.S. Northeast?
New York City

15. The Rotunda, a copy of the dome of St. Peter's Basilica, rises 272 feet high in what Pennsylvanian city on the banks of the Susquehanna River?
Harrisburg

16. The Pagoda, a resort located atop Mount Penn, is a historical landmark in what city that is well-known for its outlet shopping?
Reading

17. What city in Pennsylvania, home port of the Brig Niagara, the flagship of Commodore Perry, is home to the oldest land lighthouse on the Great Lakes?
Erie

18. What national park is mostly located on Mount Desert Island?
Acadia National Park

19. Ellis Island became part of what monument in 1965?
Statue of Liberty Monument

20.   On December 16, 1773 a group of American rebels staged what
      historic tax protest in a Massachusetts harbor?
      Boston Tea Party

21.   Early Connecticut colonists from Massachusetts were led by
      Thomas Hooker and others who established a series of permanent
      settlements, including one near what city on the Connecticut
      River in 1635?
      Hartford

22.   Name the river basin that provides water for the cities of
      Harrisburg, Williamsport, and Wilkes-Barre.
      Susquehanna River Basin

23.   In what city would you find the Library of Congress?
      Washington, D.C.

24.   Tourists travel to Connecticut to view restored whaling seaports at
      what historic shipyard that is located between the mouths of the
      Thames and Pawcatuck Rivers?
      Mystic Seaport

25.   Since it is home to more than 100 insurance companies, which
      state is known as the "insurance state?"
      Connecticut

26.   Dutch Wonderland amusement park celebrated its 50th
      anniversary in 2013. This park is in Lancaster County in which
      state?
      Pennsylvania

27.   The Taconic Range spans nearly half the border between
      Connecticut and what state?
      New York

28. The Andy Warhol Museum is a tourist attraction in what city situated where the Allegheny and Monongahela Rivers converge to form the Ohio River?
Pittsburgh

29. What city across the Thames River from New London is home to the US Naval Submarine Base?
Groton

30. The Museum Mile, well known for its museums and other fine arts institutions, is a stretch along 5th Avenue in what large city?
New York

31. What major estuary in the Northeast is one of the four most important shorebird migration sites in the world and has the second-highest concentration of seabirds in North America?
Delaware Bay

32. Settlers from what country established the first permanent European settlement in the Delaware River Valley in 1638?
Sweden

33. Name Delaware's largest city located at the junction of the Christina River and Brandywine Creek.
Wilmington

34. Rehoboth Beach, Dewey Beach, Fenwick Island, and Bethany Beach are popular getaway destinations along the coast of Delaware on what large body of water?
Atlantic Ocean

35. Cypress Swamp, home of one of the northernmost strands of cypress trees in the country, spans the border between Delaware and what U.S. state?
Maryland

36. In 1820, Maine entered the union as a free state due to a deal
     made between anti-slavery and pro-slavery states. Name this
     compromise.
     Missouri Compromise

37. In spite of a weather-related low harvest in 2004, Maine remains
     the country's leading harvester of what product?
     Blueberries

38. Cadillac Mountain, the highest point along the North Atlantic
     Coast of the United States, is located south of the town of Bar
     Harbor in what national park?
     Acadia National Park

39. Augusta, Maine is on what river?
     Kennebec River

40. Regions in river valleys along Maine's border with what Canadian
     province have allowed the state to become a large potato
     producer?
     New Brunswick

41. Which of these states does not border Maryland – Virginia,
     Delaware, New Jersey, or West Virginia?
     New Jersey

42. Wild ponies, believed to be descendants of survivors from a
     Spanish galleon that sank in the Atlantic Ocean, are found on
     what island that lies along Chincoteague Bay and is shared
     between Maryland and Virginia?
     Assateague Island

43. Name the famous Civil War battlefield that lies east of Sharpsburg
     and west of the Appalachian National Scenic Trail.
     Antietam National Battlefield

44. The 184.5-mile Chesapeake and the Ohio Canal, built between 1828 and 1850 to connect Cumberland, Maryland and Georgetown, District of Columbia, forms part of the border between Maryland and what two states?
Virginia and West Virginia

45. Francis Scott Key wrote the "Star Spangled Banner" as he watched the British invade what fort guarding Baltimore during the War of 1812?
Fort McHenry

46. In 1620, the Pilgrims crossed Cape Cod Bay and landed at what location southeast of Silver Lake?
Plymouth Rock

47. What range of hills lies east of the Taconic Range and west of Pioneer Valley in Massachusetts?
Berkshire Hills

48. Massachusetts ranks second in the production of what fruit, which is harvested by picking machines through flooded fields?
Cranberries

49. Vineyard Sound separates the Elizabeth Islands of Massachusetts from what larger island?
Martha's Vineyard

50. Which river that flows through the cities of Springfield, Holyoke, and Chicopee travels through the Pioneer Valley of Massachusetts?
Connecticut River

51. Mt. Washington in New Hampshire is known for experiencing wind speeds comparable to winds in Category 5 hurricanes and EF5 tornadoes. Mt. Washington is in what range, part of the Appalachian Mountains?
Presidential Range

52. Chocurua Lake is in which U.S. state that was the first colony to declare independence from Great Britain in 1776?
New Hampshire

53. Name the three largest cities in New Hampshire, all of which are on the Merrimack River.
Manchester, Concord, Nashua

54. What river is the largest contributor of freshwater to Chesapeake Bay?
Susquehanna River

55. The Connecticut River flows out of the mountains of New Hampshire and forms a border with what U.S. state?
Vermont

56. In 1623, the first British settlements in New Hampshire were founded along the Piscataqua River near Dover and what other city located on the coast?
Portsmouth

57. Benjamin Franklin called New Jersey a "barrel tapped at both ends" referring both to its abundant farm production and to its position between New York City and what other large city?
Philadelphia

58. On July 12th, 1967, Civil Rights riots broke out in the largest city in New Jersey. Name this city.
Newark

59. What long ridge stretches across the northwestern border of New Jersey parallel to the Delaware Water Gap National Recreational Area and contains the state's highest point, High Point?
Kittatinny Mountain

60. In 1939, Charles Darrow developed the game Monopoly. Several streets in the game, such as Boardwalk, were named after streets in what large city?
Atlantic City

61. Place these states in order according to their population densities from highest to lowest – New York, Maine, and New Jersey.
New Jersey, New York, and Maine

62. The Erie Canal, built in the 1920s, helped New York City become a worldwide trading center and opened the Midwest to development by linking the Hudson River and the Great Lakes. This canal connects Albany to what other city?
Buffalo

63. Name the lakes in New York that share their name with a national forest and are well suited for growing wine grapes.
Finger Lakes

64. Lake George, Saranac Lake, Lake Placid, and Mt. Marcy are all located in what mountain range?
Adirondack Mountains

65. Woods Hole, site of several marine institutions, is near the Elizabeth Islands and Martha's Vineyard on a cape in the easternmost part of Massachusetts. Name this cape.
Cape Cod

66. Stellwagen Bank National Marine Sanctuary, positioned at the mouth of a bay in the U.S. Northeast, is the site of upwelling of nutrient-rich water from the Gulf of Maine. Name this bay.
Massachusetts Bay

67.   The North Branch of what river begins as the outlet of Otsego
       Lake in Cooperstown, New York?
       Susquehanna River

68.   Name the canal that connects Lake Erie to Lake Ontario.
       Welland Canal

69.   Place these states in order according to their amounts of maple
       syrup production from most to least – Maine, New York, and
       Vermont.
       Vermont, New York, and Maine

70.   The U.S. Military Academy at West Point is in which state?
       New York

71.   Pittsburgh, one of the largest inland ports in the United States,
       was founded in 1758 where the Monongahela and Allegheny
       rivers merge to form what other river?
       Ohio River

72.   Amish people in Lancaster County came to Pennsylvania in the
       1700s from Germany and what other European country that
       borders France and Italy?
       Switzerland

73.   The Union Army withstood Pickett's Charge, stopping the
       advance of the South in what major Pennsylvania battle, a turning
       point during the Civil War?
       Battle of Gettysburg

74.   The near-disaster at Three Mile Island, which stopped all U.S.
       development of nuclear plants, took place near what city on the
       Susquehanna River?
       Harrisburg

75. Edwin Drake launched the petroleum industry when he drilled the first oil well in 1859 near what Pennsylvania town?
Titusville

76. Newport Harbor invites sailors of all ages to its prestigious America's Cup Yacht Race every year. Newport Harbor is on what body of water?
Narragansett Bay

77. In 1636, what Puritan freedom-seeker left Massachusetts and established the first European settlement in Rhode Island?
Roger Williams

78. The Juniata River is a tributary of what major Pennsylvania river?
Susquehanna River

79. Maryland's Monocacy River drains into what river?
Potomac River

80. Pawtucket is one of several communities in Rhode Island that are home to people from what African country, whose people have also migrated to North Dakota and Massachusetts?
Cape Verde

81. The city of Elmira, on the Chemung River, is in what state west of Massachusetts?
New York

82. In 1524, what Italian navigator was the first European explorer to visit Rhode Island?
Giovanni da Verrazzano

83. What is Rhode Island's highest point?
Jerimoth Hill

84.   The city of Hagerstown is located near what state's borders with
        West Virginia and Pennsylvania?
        Maryland

85.   In 1724, the English founded a fort near the present-day city
        of Brattleboro, near the site of the famous Battle of Bennington
        fought in New York. Name this fort.
        Fort Dummer

86.   Chincoteague Bay is shared by what two states?
        Maryland and Virginia

87.   Ethan Allen lead a force called the Green Mountain Boys that won
        fame at the battle of Fort Ticonderoga on what lake that contains
        North Hero Island and South Hero Island?
        Lake Champlain

88.   Name the state capital city in New England on the Winooski
        River.
        Montpelier

89.   One of the snowiest places in the Northeast, Jay Peak averages
        355 inches of snow each year. This mountain is near the border of
        Vermont and what Canadian province?
        Quebec

90.   The largest city in Vermont is home to Ben and Jerry's Ice Cream
        Factory. Name this city.
        Burlington

91.   The St. Croix and St. John Rivers form part of Maine's border
        with what Canadian province?
        New Brunswick

92. Name Maryland's only inhabited island not connected to the mainland by causeways or bridges, located north of Tangier Island, Virginia.
Smith Island

93. New York's Black River drains into what lake?
Lake Ontario

94. Backbone Mountain is near Maryland's border with what other state?
West Virginia

95. Flagstaff Lake can be found in what state whose border with New Hampshire is its only border with another U.S. state?
Maine

96. The Pine Barrens is the largest natural area on the Mid-Atlantic Seaboard. This region is in what state bordering New York?
New Jersey

97. Name the mountain range about 100 miles northwest of New York City that is sometimes referred to as the "First American Wilderness."
Catskill Mountains

98. You can find many preserved Victorian buildings in Cape May National Historic District in what state?
New Jersey

99. Harrisburg, Pennsylvania is on what river?
Susquehanna River

100. The bloodiest one-day battle in American History was fought at the site of what National Battlefield Monument near Sharpsburg, Maryland?
Antietam National Battlefield

101.   In 1724, the English established Fort Dummer near present-day
        Brattleboro in what state?
        Vermont

102.   President Coolidge Historic Site is in what state that is home to
        Stowe, a major ski resort?
        Vermont

103.   What Pennsylvania city, located about 30 miles northeast of
        Gettysburg, served as the nation's capital from September 1777 to
        June 1778?
        York

104.   The First Continental Congress met in Carpenters' Hall from
        September 5 to October 26, 1774 in what Pennsylvania city?
        Philadelphia

105.   Prior to Washington D.C. becoming the nation's permanent
        capital in 1790, what city served as the temporary capital of
        United States as the capital was being built?
        Philadelphia

106.   The Schuylkill River drains into the Delaware River near what city?
        Philadelphia

107.   What state became the first to ratify the Constitution on
        December 7, 1787?
        Delaware

108.   What state has the highest population density?
        New Jersey

109.   In June 2014, a proposal to build a 250-mile natural gas pipeline
        prompted a protest in the town of Windsor. This town is located
        in the Berkshire Hills in what state?
        Massachusetts

110.   What canal in southern New Jersey was built during World War II to allow U.S. ships to circumvent the German U-boats that patrolled the point where Delaware Bay meets the Atlantic Ocean?
Cape May Canal

111.   Lake Winnipesaukee is the largest lake in what state?
New Hampshire

112.   Fort McHenry National Monument and Historic Shrine is located about 19 miles from Hampton National Historic Site near what large city in Maryland?
Baltimore

113.   The North Branch River, a tributary of the Potomac River, forms part of the border between Maryland and what state?
West Virginia

114.   White Mountain National Forest spans New Hampshire and what other state?
Maine

115.   What tributary of the St. John River forms a part of the border between Maine and the Canadian provinces of New Brunswick and Quebec?
St. Francis River

116.   The Penobscot River runs through what state whose northern boundary was settled by the Webster-Ashburton Treaty?
Maine

117.   What state capital is on the St. Jones River?
Dover

118.   Name the largest and deepest of the Finger Lakes.
Seneca Lake

119.   The longest of the Finger Lakes is home to Frontenac Island.
        Name this lake.
        Cayuga Lake

120.   Name the largest lake located entirely within New York.
        Oneida Lake

121.   Fenwick Island belongs to what state?
        Delaware

122.   The Yantic and Quinebaug Rivers combine to form the Thames
        River at what city in Connecticut?
        Norwich

123.   Name the 2000-mile waterway that provides a navigable
        route along the U.S. Atlantic coast from Norfolk, Virginia
        Massachusetts, to Key West, Florida and extending along the
        Gulf of Mexico coast from Carrabelle, Florida to Brownsville,
        Texas.
        **Intracoastal Waterway (Note: It consists of the Atlantic
        Intracoastal Waterway and the Gulf Intracoastal Waterway)**

124.   What two northeastern states officially use the term
        "Commonwealth" in their names?
        Massachusetts and Pennsylvania

125.   Name the largest state in New England.
        Maine

126.   Name the most populous state in New England.
        Massachusetts

127.   Name the most densely populated state in New England.
        Rhode Island

128. Star Island, White island, and Lunging Island belong to an archipelago called the Isles of Shoals. This island group straddles between Maine and which other state?
New Hampshire

129. Mount Monadnock is located in what New England state that often appears in the writings of Ralph Waldo Emerson and Henry David Thoreau?
New Hampshire

130. Norwich, known as "The Rose of New England," is a city in what New England state that is home to the confluence of Shetucket and Yantic rivers?
Connecticut

131. Mystic Seaport, located west of the mouth of Pawcatuck River on Long Island Sound, is in what New England State?
Connecticut

132. The Assawoman Canal connects Indian River Bay to Fenwick Island in what northeastern state?
Delaware

133. Sugarloaf Mountain, part of the Longfellow Mountains, is in what state that is separated from New Brunswick by the St. Croix River?
Maine

134. The Salmon Falls River drains into the Atlantic Ocean near the town of Kittery. This town is in what northeastern state?
Maine

135. Long Lake, Churchill Lake, Eagle Lake, and Chamberlain Lake are all located on what tributary of the St. Johns River?
Allagash River

136. The town of Crisfield on Tangier Sound is located in what northeastern state?
Maryland

137. In 1790, Marblehead in Essex County was one of the ten most populous cities in the United States. Essex County is in what state?
Massachusetts

138. Monomoy Island is an 8-mile long spit of sand extending southwest from the town of Chatham in what northeastern state?
Massachusetts

139. The Berkshire Hills, west of Pioneer Valley, are in what northeastern state?
Massachusetts

140. Woods Hole, Barnstable County, and the Oceanographic Research Center on the Elizabeth Islands are all in what northeastern state?
Massachusetts

141. The town of Mystic Island is located on Great Bay south of Little Egg Harbor in what Mid-Atlantic state?
New Jersey

142. The town of Toms River is located on Barnegat Bay east of the Pine Barrens in what State?
New Jersey

143. In 1831, the first steam railroad to provide regular service began operations in New Castle in what state?
Delaware

144. Hyde Park, New York, a town with many historic sites, is located on what river?
Hudson River

145. Bangor, Maine is on what river?
Penobscot River

146. Monhegan Island, south of Acadia National Park, is in what state?
Maine

147. Name the southernmost state in New England.
Connecticut

148. Name the southernmost city on the Merrimack River in New Hampshire.
Nashua

149. Name the highest point in the Berkshire Hills of Massachusetts.
Mount Greylock

150. Chincoteague, Virginia and Ocean City, Maryland are gateways to what national seashore?
Assateague Island National Seashore

151. Eartha, a scale model of the planet Earth, currently holds the Guinness World Record for the world's largest revolving/rotating globe. This tourist attraction is on display in the city of Yarmouth in what state?
Maine

152. West Quoddy Head, the easternmost point in the contiguous United States, juts into what small body of water that separates Maine from an island group belonging to New Brunswick?
Grand Manan Channel

153. The Pocono Mountains, near Delaware Water Gap National Recreation Area, can be found in the northeastern part of what state?
Pennsylvania

154. The name of what northeastern state that is home to the Norwalk Islands comes from an Indian word meaning "on the long tidal river"?
Connecticut

155. Name the largest city in Vermont located on Lake Champlain.
Burlington

156. Monocacy National Battlefield is located south of Frederick in what northeastern state?
Maryland

157. Quaddick Reservoir, located on the Five Mile River, a tributary of the Quinebaug River, is in what state?
Connecticut

158. What is the official name of Aquidneck Island, the largest island in Narragansett Bay?
Rhode Island

159. The Twin Lakes are located southeast of Mt. Frissell near the Massachusetts border in what northeastern state?
Connecticut

160. In 1631, the town of Lewes was the site of the earliest Dutch settlements in the second-smallest state in the country. Name this state.
Delaware

161. In 1624, members of the Dutch West India Company settled on an island they called "Nutten" near what was then New Amsterdam. What is the present-day name of this island?
Governors Island

162. Tinicum Island, capital of New Sweden from 1643 to 1665, is located in the Delaware River in what state bordering New York and West Virginia?
Pennsylvania

163. "Live Free or Die" is the motto of what state that was the first colony to declare independence from Great Britain in 1776?
New Hampshire

164. Lubec, the easternmost town in the contiguous United States, is located in what state?
Maine

165. The first colonists to arrive at a Mid-Atlantic state landed on St. Clement's Island and founded the settlement of St. Mary's. Name this state.
Maryland

166. What state borders Lake Ontario and Lake Champlain?
New York

167. The Bethlehem Steel Mill, one of the first built in the country, opened in 1867 in what state?
Pennsylvania

168. The Northeast Kingdom is a region that hosts popular ski resorts such as those at Burke Mountain and Jay Peak is in what state that borders Canada?
Vermont

169.   Lanape, belonging to the Algonquin group, were the first natives
        of the area encompassing what city that is home to the Battery
        Park?
        New York City

170.   Lehigh Valley, home to the cities of Bethlehem, Allentown, and
        Easton, is a popular tourist destination in what state?
        Pennsylvania

171.   In 2002, the "First State" became the official nickname of what
        state?
        Delaware

172.   In 1883, Roselle became the first U.S. town to be lighted by
        electricity. This town is in what state?
        New Jersey

173.   During the American Revolution, which New England state
        declared independence from the original 13 colonies?
        Vermont

174.   The city of Vineland is located just east of the path of the Maurice
        River in what state?
        New Jersey

175.   The mouth of the Merrimack River is in what state?
        Massachusetts

CHAPTER 2

U.S. Midwest

1. Galena, a city located east of the Upper Mississippi River National Wildlife and Fish Refuge, is a major lead producer in the northwestern part of which state?
    Illinois

2. Which state extends farther north – Iowa or Illinois?
    Iowa

3. Which state extends farther south – Illinois or Missouri?
    Missouri

4. Which midwestern state extends farther east – Michigan or Ohio?
    Ohio

5. Which state does not border Wisconsin – Michigan, Indiana, or Iowa?
    Indiana

6. What High Plains state borders Kansas to the north?
    Nebraska

7. What state that has Grand Lake St. Marys as its largest lake borders Indiana to the east?
    Ohio

8. Name the aquifer system in the High Plains region that extends from Texas to South Dakota.
    Ogallala Aquifer

9. Kearney, Nebraska is on what river?
    Platte River

10. The first Europeans that explored the area of Illinois in 1673 arrived via the Mississippi River and what other major river?
    Ohio River

11.   The Mayo Clinic, a leader in medical care, has a research center in Rochester, a city in what midwestern state?
      Minnesota

12.   Kings Island, claimed to be the largest amusement and water park in the Midwest, is located about 21 miles north of what city in Ohio?
      Cincinnati

13.   What city was founded in the late 1790s when Jean Baptiste du Sable, a black trapper and trader, built a cabin on marshy land along a river near Lake Michigan?
      Chicago

14.   What Illinois city, located on an island in the Mississippi River, served as the state capital when it was settled by French and Indian traders in 1881?
      Kaskaskia

15.   The Sturgis Motorcycle Rally is a large event in what state that is home to Custer State Park?
      South Dakota

16.   What city, established by the French in the 1700s, was the first permanent white settlement in Indiana?
      Vincennes

17.   The Coteau des Prairie Region lies mostly in what state?
      South Dakota

18.   The U.S. center of population in 1900 was located just east of the city of Columbus in what state that borders Lake Michigan and the Ohio River?
      Indiana

19.   Name the smallest state in the contiguous United States west of
        the Appalachian Mountains?
        Indiana

20.   The Big Darby Creek National Scenic River is in which state that
        is home to Niles, President McKinley's birthplace?
        Ohio

21.   Eau Claire is a city in what state bordering Michigan and Iowa?
        Wisconsin

22.   James Whitcomb and Theodore Dreiser are poets that hail from
        what Indiana city on the Wabash River?
        Terre Haute

23.   The National Underground Railroad Freedom Center is located in
        what city that is linked to Covington, Kentucky by the historic
        Roebling Bridge?
        Cincinnati

24.   Grand Portage National Monument is a reminder of the role
        played by the Ojibwe Indians in the North American fur trade in
        the 1800s in what state?
        Minnesota

25.   Sturgeon Bay, a town rich in maritime heritage, is nestled
        between the waters of Lake Michigan and Green Bay on what
        peninsula?
        Door Peninsula

26.   Mount Baldy is the largest sand dune in Indiana Dunes National
        Lakeshore, located just west of Michigan City on what large body
        of water?
        Lake Michigan

27. Upper Red Lake and Lower Red Lake are located in what state?
Minnesota

28. Effigy Mounds National Monument is located just west of Marquette, northeast Iowa along the Wisconsin border on what river?
Mississippi River

29. Which city is farther west – Sioux City, Iowa or International Falls, Minnesota?
Sioux City, Iowa

30. Des Moines is located at the confluence of the Des Moines River and what other river?
Raccoon River

31. Hawkeye Point, the highest point in Iowa, is located south of the border with what state?
Minnesota

32. Devils Lake, well-known for its harvest of perch, is in which state west of Minnesota?
North Dakota

33. Which city is farther north – Grand Portage, Minnesota or Sault Ste. Marie, Michigan?
Grand Portage, Minnesota

34. The city of Marshalltown is located west of a German communal society known as the Amana Colonies in what state?
Iowa

35. Whitefish Point, home to Great Lakes Shipwreck Museum, is located near the southeastern tip of what lake?
Lake Superior

36.   The Marblehead Peninsula, Ohio, forms the northern shore of
       what bay?
       Sandusky Bay

37.   Manitoulin Island in Lake Huron is the largest island in the Great
       Lakes. Name the second largest island in the Great Lakes, known
       for attracting visitors to the Michigan-owned waters of Lake
       Superior.
       Isle Royale

38.   The city of Dubuque, near Julian Dubuque Monument, is situated
       on the Mississippi River near the point where Iowa meets Illinois
       and what other state?
       Wisconsin

39.   Wine tasting in the vineyards of the Leelanau Peninsula attracts
       tourists to the area north of Traverse City in what state?
       Michigan

40.   Name all the Great Lakes that border at least four U.S. states?
       Lake Michigan and Lake Erie

41.   The Cimarron River makes its first entry into Kansas from what
       neighboring state?
       Colorado

42.   Name the second-largest freshwater island in the U.S. after Isle
       Royale.
       Drummond Island

43.   You can still find reddish-pink pipestone in Pipestone National
       Monument, a tourist attraction in what state?
       Minnesota

44. What peninsula in Michigan, sometimes known as the Copper Country, is the departure point for ferries traveling to Isle Royal National Park?
Keweenaw Peninsula

45. The Republican River enters Nebraska from what neighboring state?
Kansas

46. Dodge City, Kansas traces its history back to Fort Dodge, a settlement built in 1865 on what major trail?
Santa Fe Trail

47. Motown Museum preserves the music legacy of what city located between Lake St. Claire and Lake Erie?
Detroit

48. Wichita, Kansas is located on what river?
Arkansas River

49. The town of Lindsborg, home to a large number of Swedish descendants, is home to the Anatoly Karpov International School of Chess in what state?
Kansas

50. The Magnificent Mile, famous for its shopping malls, can be found in what midwestern city?
Chicago

51. Holland, Michigan, well-known for its rich history and Dutch-American population, is on the eastern shore of what lake?
Lake Michigan

52. Dubuque, Iowa, is close to the junction of what two states?
Wisconsin and Illinois

53.   In 1814, German Lutherans established the town of New
        Harmony on the banks of the Wabash River in what state?
        Indiana

54.   The town of Winterset, known for being the birthplace of John
        Wayne, is the seat of Madison County in what state bordered by
        Wisconsin and Nebraska?
        Iowa

55.   What canal, completed in 1825, made it easier for settlers to
        reach the area around Michigan?
        Erie Canal

56.   Madeline Island is the heart of Ojibwe heritage and spirituality.
        This island is in which state?
        Wisconsin

57.   The Dakota Territory, formed in 1861, was made up of parts of
        what two other territories?
        Minnesota and Nebraska Territories

58.   Spirit Lake Dakota Nation can be found near Devil's Lake, Dry
        Lake, and Sweetwater Lake in what midwestern state?
        North Dakota

59.   What midwestern state got its name from the Iroquois word *ohi-
        yo'* meaning "great river"?
        Ohio

60.   In 1874, a military expedition led by General George Armstrong
        Custer discovered the existence of gold in what elevated region
        sacred to the Lakota?
        Black Hills

61. Grand Traverse Bay is to Lake Michigan as Thunder Bay is to what?
Lake Huron

62. The town of Fort Riley was established in 1853 to protect settlers along the Oregon and Santa Fe Trails. Fort Riley is in what state often referred to as "the Wheat Capital of the World"?
Kansas

63. In 1673, French explorers Louis Joliet and Jacques Marquette became the first Europeans to visit which midwestern territory which originally had no port on the Great Lakes?
Illinois Territory

64. The Keweenaw Peninsula is separated from what island by a 100-mile water trail used by canoers?
Isle Royale

65. Name the bridge that has linked Michigan's peninsulas since 1957.
Mackinac Bridge

66. The Sheyenne River flows through West Fargo, North Dakota before draining into what larger river?
Red River of the North

67. The Soo Locks, among the busiest shipping lanes in the Western Hemisphere, are near the city of Sault Ste. Marie on Michigan's Upper Peninsula. Sault Ste. Marie is located on what river?
St. Mary's River

68. What mountain range in Superior National Forest is famous for its open pit iron ore mines?
Mesabi Range

69. Tom Sauk Mountain, near the source of the St. Francis River, is the highest point in what state?
Missouri

70. What point, located west of Lake of the Woods in Red Lake Indian Reservation, is the northernmost point of the 48 contiguous states?
Northwest Angle

71. Name the lake that is the source of the Mississippi River.
Lake Itasca

72. What strait system links Lake Michigan and Lake Huron?
Straits of Mackinac

73. The Boundary Waters Canoe Area Wilderness is located near Minnesota's border with what Canadian province?
Ontario

74. What site near St. Louis was the starting point of Lewis and Clark's Corps of Discovery?
Camp Wood

75. The Corps of Discovery was commissioned by Thomas Jefferson to seek a route to what ocean?
Pacific Ocean

76. What city in Missouri is well-known for its country music shows that bring many tourists to the Ozark Mountains?
Branson

77. Lake Winnebago is to Wisconsin as Lake Winnibigoshish is to what?
Minnesota

78. The boyhood home of author Mark Twain is located near Hannibal, Missouri on what river?
Mississippi River

79. The U.S. center of population has moved from Kent County, Maryland in 1790 to Texas County as of 2010. Texas County is in what state that borders Illinois and Arkansas?
Missouri

80. What national forest in Missouri consists of four zones and is named for a well-known author?
Mark Twain National Forest

81. What structural monument, the tallest in the United States, was designed by Eero Saarinen and completed in 1965?
The Gateway Arch

82. What region of grass-covered, stabilized sand dunes covers 20,000 square miles of plains in parts of Nebraska and South Dakota?
The Sand Hills

83. Which Minnesotan lake is farther north – Upper Red Lake or Mille Lacs Lake?
Upper Red Lake

84. What tributary of the Missouri River flows through the entire northern part of the Sand Hills in Nebraska?
Niobrara River

85. What Nebraska City is the largest processor of meats and meat products in the country?
Omaha

86.   Which region in Kansas extends farthest north – the Flint Hills
        or the Smoky Hills?
        Smoky Hills

87.   What prominent column of clay and sandstone in the state of
        Nebraska was a beacon for travelers on the Oregon and Mormon
        Trails?
        Chimney Rock

88.   The Republican River flows south from Nebraska and joins what
        river near Junction City, Kansas to form the Kansas River?
        Smoky Hill River

89.   Jewel Cave National Monument can be found in what national
        forest in South Dakota?
        Black Hills National Forest

90.   The city of Grand Island is located in what state?
        Nebraska

91.   What river that begins in Lake Traverse Indian Reservation drains
        into the Missouri River near Sioux Falls, South Dakota?
        Big Sioux River

92.   Name the dam on the Missouri River that generates electricity
        and provides water for irrigation to large parts of North Dakota.
        Garrison Dam

93.   Grahams Island State Park is located in North Dakota's largest
        natural lake. Name this lake.
        Devils Lake

94.   Name the national park located in the North Dakota Badlands.
        Theodore Roosevelt National Park

95. The historic Mandan and Hidatsa Villages, where Sacagawea joined the Lewis and Clark expedition in the spring of 1805, are located near which present day North Dakota town on the Missouri River?
Washburn

96. The St. Joseph River and St. Mary's River join to form what river near Fort Wayne, Indiana?
Maumee River

97. The Hennepin Canal joins the Illinois River and what other river?
Mississippi River

98. The geographic center of North America is southwest of what town in North Dakota?
Rugby

99. Akron, Ohio is the chief rubber-producing city in the United States, giving it its nickname, "the Rubber Capital of the World." Akron is located on a tributary of what river that empties into Lake Erie?
Cuyahoga River

100. What city in Ohio is located near the junction of the Ohio River and the Little Miami River?
Cincinnati

101. Leavenworth, site of a U.S. federal prison, is in what state bordering the Missouri River?
Kansas

102. What city in Indiana, not far from the Ohio border, is near the junction of the St. Joseph and the St. Mary Rivers?
Fort Wayne

103.   Marion, site of a U.S. federal prison, is north of Shawnee National
        Forest in what state?
        Illinois

104.   The Osage River drains into the Missouri River near what state
        capital?
        Jefferson City

105.   Midway International Airport is to Chicago, Illinois as Hopkins
        International Airport is to what?
        Cleveland, Ohio

106.   Name Ohio's sole national forest, located near the Ohio River.
        Wayne National Forest

107.   Fort Pierre National Grassland can be found in what state?
        South Dakota

108.   Mount Sunflower, the highest point in Kansas, is near the border
        with what state?
        Colorado

109.   What state is made up of two regions: The Till Plains in the west
        and the Allegheny Plateau in the east?
        Ohio

110.   The cities of East Chicago, Michigan City, and Gary are in what
        state bordering the Ohio River on its southern border?
        Indiana

111.   In 1794, Indian resistance to the United States' claim to the
        Northwest Territory came to a halt when the Indians were
        defeated at the Battle of Fallen Timbers in which midwestern
        state?
        Ohio

112. Name the memorial in the Black Hills of South Dakota, built to resemble a famous Lakota chief that honors the culture, tradition, and living heritage of Great Plains Indian tribes.
Crazy Horse National Memorial

113. The city of Valparaiso, well-known for its university, is in what state, the southernmost on Lake Michigan?
Indiana

114. Name the national monument home to a famous public work of art that was designed by Gutzon Borglum and nicknamed the "Shrine of Democracy" shortly after its completion.
Mount Rushmore National Monument

115. Bedford, Indiana, the "Limestone Capital of the World," is south of Monroe Lake, which forms part of the border of what national forest?
Hoosier National Forest

116. The Corn Palace in Mitchell is a testament to the importance of agriculture in what state?
South Dakota

117. Eagle Mountain is the highest point in what state?
Minnesota

118. The town of Quincy, on the Mississippi River, is south of Mark Twain National Wildlife Refuge in what state whose largest lake is Carlyle Lake?
Illinois

119. The town of Deadwood, established in 1876, is located in what midwestern state?
South Dakota

120. The village of Tampico, President Reagan's birthplace, is in what
      state?
      Illinois

121. The Sturgis Motorcycle Rally is a well-known event in what
      midwestern state?
      South Dakota

122. Big Stone Lake is the source of what tributary of the Mississippi
      River?
      Minnesota River

123. The city of Pierre, South Dakota is south of what large reservoir?
      Lake Oahe

124. Name the smallest contiguous state west of the Appalachian
      Mountains.
      Indiana

125. Independence, Missouri is located just east of what large city?
      Kansas City

126. Name the city northeast of Table Rock Lake that is Missouri's
      center of country music.
      Branson

127. What large man-made lake was created by the building of
      Garrison Dam, North Dakota?
      Lake Sakakawea

128. Name the island belonging to Michigan that is situated between
      St. Joseph Island and Cockburn Island, Ontario.
      Drummond Island

129. What national park includes parts of Rainy Lake along the
      Minnesota/Ontario border?
      Voyageurs National Park

130. Name the lake north of Big Stone Lake along the South Dakota-
      Minnesota border.
      Lake Traverse

131. The St. Louis River drains into a bay near two ports, one in
      Wisconsin and the other in Minnesota. Name these ports.
      Duluth, Minnesota and Superior, Wisconsin

132. The Driftless Area, an area that includes rugged hills and steep
      topography, extends into Iowa, Illinois, and Minnesota, but is
      primarily in the southwest part of which state?
      Wisconsin

133. What midwestern state is a leader in nuclear power production in
      the United States?
      Illinois

134. Shawnee National Forest in southern Illinois is drained by what
      river?
      Ohio River

135. The St. Clair River, Lake St. Clair, and what other waterway link
      Lake Erie and Lake Huron?
      Detroit River

136. The Bad River Indian Reservation is located on Wisconsin's
      largest island. Name this island.
      Madeline Island

137. What midwestern state borders the most number of Great Lakes?
      Michigan

138.   William Howard Taft National Historic site is in what state that
       is home to the world's largest Amish population?
       Ohio

139.   What national forest spans Montana and South Dakota and is one
       of the gateways to Yellowstone National Park?
       Custer National Forest

140.   Wisconsin's most populous river island, French Island, is located
       just north of the city of La Crosse in what river?
       Mississippi River

141.   The St. Clair River flows from what Great Lake?
       Lake Huron

142.   Barbed wire was invented in DeKalb, a city in what state that is
       also home to the Vermilion National Wild and Scenic River?
       Illinois

143.   Wisconsin's most populous lake island is located in the
       northeastern part of the state. Name this island.
       Washington Island

144.   The Niobrara National Scenic Riverway is in what state?
       Nebraska

145.   What large city in southeastern Wisconsin derives its name from
       the Algonquian word for "beautiful land"?
       Milwaukee

146.   The city of Beloit is located near Wisconsin's border with what
       state to the south?
       Illinois

147. What canal, operated by the U.S. Army Corps of Engineers, connects Lake Huron to Lake Superior?
St. Mary's Canal (Soo Canal)

148. Michigan City is just northeast of what national lakeshore?
Indiana Dunes National Lakeshore

149. Granite City, Illinois is part of the larger metropolitan area of what city on the Mississippi River?
St. Louis

150. Saginaw Bay, Michigan, is a large bay in what body of water?
Lake Huron

151. Desoto National Wildlife Refuge is located on what river near Iowa's border with Nebraska?
Missouri River

152. What national wildlife refuge in Kansas is located southeast of Emporia along the Neosho River?
Flint Hills National Wildlife Refuge

153. The second largest Great Lake is the only one that directly receives water flow from two other Great Lakes. Name this lake.
Lake Huron

154. Ely is a town in Superior National Forest in the northeastern part of what state?
Minnesota

155. Sleeping Bear Dunes National Lakeshore is located on what lake that shares its name with a midwestern state?
Lake Michigan

156.   Little Missouri National Grassland, the largest grassland in the
        United States, is home to White Butte, the highest point in what
        state?
        North Dakota

157.   In 1836, the midwestern town of Bronson was renamed
        Kalamazoo. This modern-day city is located in what state?
        Michigan

158.   The city of Aurora, southwest of Naperville, is situated on the Fox
        River. Fox River is a tributary of what larger river?
        Illinois River

159.   Lake Pepin borders Minnesota and which state to the east?
        Wisconsin

160.   Lake Darling is formed by damming what river that joins the Des
        Lacs River near Minot, North Dakota?
        Souris River (Mouse River)

161.   The shores of which lake can be found in Minnesota's Voyageurs
        National Park – Rainy Lake or Lake Superior?
        Rainy Lake

162.   Ohio's only national park, Cuyahoga Valley National Park, is
        adjacent to what large city near Cuyahoga Falls?
        Akron

163.   Normal is a city just north of what large city in Illinois?
        Bloomington

164.   Name the city in Michigan situated where the St. Clair River
        flows out of Lake Huron.
        Port Huron

165. South Point Village, the southernmost point in Ohio, is near the location where Ohio converges with Kentucky and what other state?
West Virginia

166. Lincoln Home National Historic Site is to Illinois as Lincoln Boyhood National Memorial is to what?
Indiana

167. Joplin, Missouri was the scene of a major tornado in 2011. This city is near the border between Kansas and what other state?
Oklahoma

168. Harry S. Truman National Historic Site can be found in what city, east of Kansas City, Missouri?
Independence

169. The historic Battle of Fallen Timbers was fought near what suburb of Toledo, Ohio that shares its name with a major river in the region?
Maumee

170. Kenosha, a city on Lake Michigan, is in which state?
Wisconsin

171. What national park encompasses part of Namakan Lake and forms part of the border between Minnesota and Ontario?
Voyageurs National Park

172. The Pine Ridge escarpment extends into South Dakota's Pine Ridge Indian Reservation and the northern section of Wyoming's Niobrara River watershed from what state?
Nebraska

173. Name Ohio's largest island.
South Bass Island

174. Minuteman Missile National Historic Site is located about 6 miles east of the town of Wall in what state bordering Wyoming and Minnesota?
South Dakota

175. Sioux Falls is located near the point where the Big Sioux River begins to form the border between South Dakota and what other state?
Iowa

CHAPTER 3

U.S. Southwest

1. Ship Rock, also known as Tsé Bit a í, or "the winged rock" in Navajo, is a volcanic landform in the northwestern part of what state?
New Mexico

2. What state borders the Mexican state of Sonora and Texas?
New Mexico

3. What state borders Arkansas and Colorado?
Oklahoma

4. What state is bordered by New Mexico to the east?
Arizona

5. What U.S. state borders the Mexican state of Nuevo Leon?
Texas

6. What river drains into the Rio Grande River just west of Amistad Reservoir, Texas?
Pecos River

7. What southwestern state is the youngest of the 48 contiguous states?
Arizona

8. Chaco Culture National Historical Park is in what state that is home to the historic city of Clovis near its border with Texas?
New Mexico

9. Sam Houston National Forest is in what state?
Texas

10. The Cibola National Forest and Grasslands are located in Texas, Oklahoma, and what state that is bordered by both these states to the east?
New Mexico

11.   The Concho River runs through the heart of San Angelo in what
       state?
       Texas

12.   The source of the Brazos River is in what state?
       New Mexico

13.   The Coronado National Forest spans New Mexico and what state
       to the west?
       Arizona

14.   The Tulsa Air and Space Museum can be found in what state?
       Oklahoma

15.   The Heard Museum has the premier collection of Native
       American art and culture in the country. This is located in which
       southwestern city that is home to the Sky Harbor International
       Airport?
       Phoenix

16.   Port Arthur is a Gulf Coast city on the shores of Sabine Lake in
       what state?
       Texas

17.   Glen Canyon Dam is built on the Colorado River in the northern
       part of what state?
       Arizona

18.   What national park is home to the highest point in Texas?
       Guadalupe Mountains National Park

19.   Petrified Forest National Park is in what state?
       Arizona

20.   Bandera, Kerrville, and Fredericksburg are towns in what rugged
        Texas region populated mostly by cacti and scrub trees?
        Hill Country

21.   Name the largest city in Arizona on the Colorado River
        Yuma

22.   What Texan city on the Colorado River is nicknamed the "Live
        Music Capital of the World"?
        Austin

23.   Gallup, New Mexico is the largest Indian center in the southwest.
        This town is about 25 miles east of what bordering state?
        Arizona

24.   Sugar Land, Texas is located southwest of what large city?
        Houston

25.   Farmington, New Mexico is situated on what river that rises in
        Colorado and drains into the Colorado River in Utah?
        San Juan River

26.   Guadalupe Mountains National Park is home to a fossil reef from
        the Permian Period. This park is located southwest of Carlsbad
        Caverns National Park, New Mexico in what bordering state?
        Texas

27.   Dallas and Fort Worth are cities on what river?
        Trinity River

28.   You can visit the Museum of the Great Plains in Lawton, a city in
        what state that is bordered by Kansas and Colorado to the north?
        Oklahoma

29. The world's first atomic bomb was tested on July 16, 1945 at Trinity Site in the White Sands Missile Range. This range is located in the northern part of what segment of the southern Rocky Mountains?
San Andres Mountains

30. The Tumacácori National Historical Park is located in Tumacacori about 18 miles north of Nogales in which state?
Arizona

31. The world's largest field of gypsum sand dunes can be found in what national monument west of Alamogordo, New Mexico?
White Sands National Monument

32. Name all the states on the Trail of Tears National Historic Trail.
Alabama, Arkansas, Georgia, Illinois, Kentucky, Missouri, North Carolina, Oklahoma, and Tennessee

33. Glendale, Arizona is closest to what city – Phoenix or Tempe?
Phoenix

34. Emory Peak is the highest peak in the Chisos Mountain Range in what Texas national park that is populated mostly by Chihuahua Desert vegetation?
Big Bend National Park

35. What is the most prominent flora in many national preserves in Arizona?
Cactus

36. Nacogdoches, a city near Angelina National Forest, claims to be the oldest town in what state?
Texas

37. The Indian Removal Act of 1830 mandated the western displacement of all American Indian tribes living to the east of what river?
Mississippi River

38. Vermillion Cliffs National Monument and Coconino National Forest are in what state?
Arizona

39. Saguaro National Park is accessible from what large city in Arizona?
Tucson

40. The Mora River flows through Las Vegas National Wildlife Refuge at the edge of llano Estacado in what state that borders the Mexican state of Chihuahua?
New Mexico

41. Eufaula Lake, Oklahoma's largest lake, is located on what river?
Canadian River

42. Sabine Lake is located at the confluence of Sabine River and what other river?
Neches River

43. Port Mansfield Channel is at the southern boundary of what national seashore in Texas?
Padre Island National Seashore

44. Grand Lake O' the Cherokees is located on what river in northeastern Oklahoma?
Neosho

45. Name the largest of New Mexico's nineteen Indian pueblos.
Zuni pueblo

46. Lubbock and Amarillo are cities in the Llano Estacado region, which spans Texas and what other state?
New Mexico

47. Name the Indian tribe In Arizona, known for their pottery and unique carved kachinas, whose members reside on a reservation that is entirely surrounded by the Navajo Indian Reservation.
Hopi

48. Padre Island is bounded to the north by what eighteen-mile-long barrier island located between Corpus Christi and the Gulf of Mexico?
Mustang Island

49. Fort Smith National Historic site spans Arkansas and what other state?
Oklahoma

50. Davis Dam, near Bullhead City, Arizona, dams the Colorado River to create what lake?
Lake Mojave

51. The Virgin River rises in Utah and drains into the Colorado River near what lake east of Las Vegas?
Lake Mead

52. What river whose headwaters are near Fayetteville, Arkansas flows through southern Missouri before reentering Arkansas?
White River

53. On September 28, 1838, Cherokee leader John Benge led 1,079 natives from Fort Payne, Alabama to present-day Stillwell in what state?
Oklahoma

54.   Aransas National Wildlife Refuge is near the town of Austwell in
       what state?
       Texas

55.   Sam Houston National Forest and Davy Crockett National Forest
       are in what state?
       Texas

56.   What desert extends into the lower elevation regions of northwest
       Arizona?
       Mojave Desert

57.   What river drains into San Antonio Bay in the Gulf of Mexico?
       Guadalupe River

58.   The National Cowboy and Western Heritage Museum is in what
       southwestern state?
       Oklahoma

59.   Organ Pipe Cactus National Monument is in what state?
       Arizona

60.   What city located in the center of the Texas Panhandle is
       the gateway to Palo Duro Canyon, America's second-largest
       canyon?
       Amarillo

61.   Togiak National Wildlife Refuge is to Alaska as Wichita
       Mountains Wildlife Refuge is to what?
       Oklahoma

62.   The Cimarron River flows through the panhandle of what state?
       Oklahoma

63. What rugged escarpment in Arizona forms the southern limit of the Colorado Plateau?
Mogollon Rim

64. Sonoran Desert National Monument and Kofa National Wildlife Refuge are in what state?
Arizona

65. Name the largest city in the Chihuahuan Desert, the second largest desert in the United States.
El Paso

66. The longest tributary of the Arkansas River flows through several states including Oklahoma. Name this river.
Canadian River

67. Truth or Consequences, New Mexico is on what river?
Rio Grande

68. Ponca City is a small city on the edges of Osage Nation Reservation in which state – New Mexico or Oklahoma?
Oklahoma

69. Which state does not border Oklahoma – Missouri, Arkansas or Louisiana?
Louisiana

70. Washita Battlefield National Historic Site marks the location where Lt. George Armstrong Custer's 7th Cavalry attacked Black Kettle's Southern Cheyenne camp on the Washita River in Oklahoma. This river rises in the panhandle of what bordering state?
Texas

71. The western end of the Ouachita Mountains is in what state?
Oklahoma

72. What city in Texas is located near the junction of the Elm Fork and West Fork of the Trinity River?
Irving

73. What river flows west to east past Black Mesa, the highest point in Oklahoma?
Cimarron River

74. Lake Tawakoni, east of Garland, Texas, is the source of what river?
Sabine River

75. The Stockton Plateau, bordered by the Pecos River to the east, is a physical region in what state?
Texas

76. The town of Roswell is on the Rio Hondo near its confluence with the Pecos River. This town is in what state?
New Mexico

77. Pecos National Historic Park is southeast of what state capital?
Santa Fe

78. The Cimarron River drains into the Arkansas River near Keystone Lake in which state?
Oklahoma

79. What Mexican state shares a 25-mile border with New Mexico?
Sonora

80. Chamizal National Memorial is located in what city in the Chihuahuan Desert of Texas?
El Paso

CHAPTER 4

U.S. West

1.   As an alternative to the dangerous Oregon Trail, some pioneers
      explored a new route that went through the southern mountains
      of the Cascade Range and the deserts of Nevada before passing
      Goose Lake, Tule Lake, and Lower Klamath Lake at the California-
      Oregon border. Name this trail.
      Applegate Trail

2.   Which contiguous state extends farthest west?
      Washington

3.   Which state does not border Idaho – Colorado or Montana?
      Colorado

4.   Which state does not border Wyoming – Idaho or North Dakota?
      North Dakota

5.   Which state borders Nevada to the north – Oregon or Utah?
      Oregon

6.   Which state borders Montana – South Dakota or Nebraska?
      South Dakota

7.   What state extends farthest north?
      Alaska

8.   Which western state of the 48 contiguous states extends farthest
      north?
      Washington

9.   Which state is in the Mountain Time Zone – Utah or Oregon?
      Utah

10.   Parts of which state share the Hawaii-Aleutian Time Zone with
      Hawaii?
      Alaska

11. Utah and what other state border Wyoming to the south?
     Colorado

12. Name the only U.S. state that borders the Canadian province of
     Alberta.
     Montana

13. Which state extends farther south – Nevada or Utah?
     Nevada

14. What U.S. state extends farthest west?
     Alaska

15. Which state is not located in the contiguous United States –
     Colorado, Hawaii, or Washington?
     Hawaii

16. Mt. Isto is the highest point of the world's highest mountain
     range located entirely within the Arctic Circle. Name this range.
     Brooks Range

17. Soda Springs, originally called "Beer Springs" by explorers and
     settlers, is located at the junction of the California and Oregon
     Trails in what state?
     Idaho

18. Mt. McKinley is in what mountain range?
     Alaska Range

19. Heceta Head Lighthouse and Lightkeeper's Home in the Siuslaw
     National Forest is the most photographed site along the coast of
     what state that shares the Columbia Plateau with Washington and
     Idaho?
     Oregon

20. The National Elk Refuge can be found in what state?
    Wyoming

21. Name the largest city on the island of Hawaii?
    Hilo

22. Sauvie Island is the largest island in the Columbia River, which rises in the northern Cascade Range in what Canadian province?
    British Columbia

23. Ely is a city situated in the foothills of Egan Range in what state?
    Nevada

24. Bald Mountain is a ski resort near Ketchum in what state?
    Idaho

25. Honolulu is on what island?
    O'ahu

26. What dam near the Black Mountains protects California's Imperial Valley from spring floods and seasonal droughts?
    Hoover Dam

27. What lake was formed behind Glen Canyon Dam?
    Lake Powell

28. The Makah Museum honors the famous sea-faring peoples of the Pacific Northwest. This museum is located in Neah Bay in what state?
    Washington

29. Lahaina, the former Hawaiian royal capital, is on what island?
    Maui

30. The Pribilof Islands belong to what state?
    Alaska

31. The Powder River drains into the Yellowstone River in what state?
Montana

32. Boulder City is located southwest of Lake Mead in what state?
Nevada

33. What river that rises in the Gates of the Arctic National Park drains into Kotzebue Sound?
Kobuk River

34. Hovenweep National Monument is home to a group of five ancient ruins spanning southwestern Colorado and the southeastern part of which state?
Utah

35. In 1941, President Roosevelt created what refuge on the second largest island in the United States?
Kodiak National Wildlife Refuge

36. The famous Na Pali Coast is located on what Hawaiian island?
Kauai

37. Kotor, Montenegro and Toba City, Japan are two sister cities of what California city, sometimes referred to as the "American Riviera," that is home to the world-famous Stearns Wharf?
Santa Barbara

38. What city served as the capital of Spanish and Mexican California between 1776 and 1849?
Monterrey

39.   In 2007, Natural Bridges National Monument was named the
        world's first international dark-sky park, with almost no light
        pollution. This monument is in the southeastern part of what
        state?
        Utah

40.   The George C. Page Museum is located at the site of the La Brea
        Tar Pits in what city?
        Los Angeles

41.   What Alaskan mountain range continues to undergo
        topographical changes as a result of the consistent shifting of a
        fault located in Prince William Sound?
        Chugach Mountains

42.   On April 18, 1906, a major earthquake shook what large city in
        the western United States?
        San Francisco

43.   The area around the city of Gillette is known for its abundance
        of low sulfur coal. Gillette is located in what state that borders
        Montana and Idaho?
        Wyoming

44.   The northernmost main Hawaiian island is sometimes known as
        the Garden Island. Name this island.
        Kauai

45.   Sawtooth National Forest is shared by Utah and what state?
        Idaho

46.   Kate's Needle is the highest point in what mountain range whose
        peaks form a border between Alaska and British Columbia?
        Coast Mountains

47. In 1805, Lewis and Clark camped near present-day Lolo in the Northern Rocky Mountains of Montana. This town is located near what city at the confluence of the Clark Fork, Bitterroot, and Blackfoot Rivers?
Missoula

48. Hana Highway is a well-travelled road on what Hawaiian island?
Maui

49. Kings Canyon National Park, California borders what national park to its south?
Sequoia National Park

50. The headquarters of Dixie National Forest, which straddles the divide between the Great Basin and the Colorado River watershed, are located in Cedar City in what state?
Utah

51. Cape Wrangell, the westernmost point of United States, is on what Alaskan island?
Attu

52. The city of St. George is often referred to as "Utah's Dixie" because of its temperate climate. This city provides an access point to what national park?
Zion National Park

53. Oceanside, California is well-known for its Cape Cod-style harbor village. This city is the northern terminus for many roads that provide access to what larger city to the south?
San Diego

54. The city of Lewiston is in what state that borders Washington and Oregon?
Idaho

55.   You can find granite monoliths such as Half Dome and El Capitan
       in what U.S. national park?
       Yosemite National Park

56.   The Riverside Metropolitan Museum is a tourist attraction in
       Riverside, California. This city forms a conurbation area with
       what city to the northeast?
       San Bernardino

57.   The Diamond on Longs Peak is a famous rock climb in what
       national park in Colorado?
       Rocky Mountain National Park

58.   Capitol Reef National Park and Dixie National Forest are in what
       state?
       Utah

59.   Mt. Baker-Snoqualmie National Forest is accessible from the city
       of Bellingham in what state?
       Washington

60.   Mount Blackburn is the highest point in what mountain range in
       eastern Alaska?
       Wrangell Mountains

61.   Mount Marcus Baker is the highest point in what mountain
       range that extends into the Wrangell-St. Elias National Park and
       Preserve in Alaska?
       Chugach Mountains

62.   The Port of Dutch Harbor is considered first in the nation in
       terms of the quantity of catch landed. This port is located on
       Amaknak Island in what city, one of the largest in the Aleutian
       chain.
       Unalaska

63. What river rises in Glacier National Park and flows through the Canadian Province of Alberta before reentering Montana and draining into the Missouri River near Fort Peck Lake?
Milk River

64. Borah Peak, the highest point in the Lost River Range, is also the highest point in what state?
Idaho

65. Lamar, Colorado is on what river that flows eastward into Kansas and eventually drains into the Mississippi River?
Arkansas River

66. The Lewis and Clark Range is a subsection of the Rocky Mountains in what state bordering Wyoming and the Canadian Province of Saskatchewan?
Montana

67. Brigham City is located in what state bordering Idaho and Colorado?
Utah

68. Between 1772 and 1775, the Russians set up a permanent settlement at the Aleut village of Iliuliuk near what present day city?
Unalaska

69. Kenai, Alaska is on what inlet of the Gulf of Alaska?
Cook Inlet

70. Pu'ukohola Heiau National Historic Site is on what Hawaiian island?
Hawaii (Big Island)

71. Name the United States' largest national park.
Wrangell-St. Elias National Park

72.   The headwaters of the Colorado River are in what national park?
       Rocky Mountain National Park

73.   Kobuk Valley National Park is in what state?
       Alaska

74.   A bi-national park system on the border between the Yukon
       Territory, the province of British Columbia, and the U.S. state of
       Alaska is home to the largest non-polar ice field in the world and
       is a UNESCO World Heritage Site. This park system consists of
       the Kluane National Park in the Yukon, Tatshenshini in British
       Columbia, and what two parks in Alaska?
       Glacier Bay and Wrangell-St. Elias National Parks

75.   Name the only dam on the Colorado River in Mexico that is the
       last in a long line of dams including Hoover Dam and Davis
       Dam.
       Morelos Dam

76.   The Harding Icefield, the largest ice field entirely within the
       United States, is located in what national park?
       Kenai Fjords National Park

77.   Mount Whitney, the highest peak in the mainland United States,
       is in what mountain range?
       Sierra Nevada

78.   Parts of seven U.S. states are in the Colorado River Basin. Name
       them.
       **Colorado, Wyoming, Utah, New Mexico, Nevada, Arizona
       and California**

79.   The Coachella Canal diverts water from the Colorado River near
       Yuma, Arizona to Riverside in what U.S. state?
       California

80. The U.S.S. Arizona Memorial is on what Hawaiian island?
O'ahu

81. Name the northwestern most point of the mainland, contiguous United States.
Cape Flattery

82. Bear Lake borders Utah and which state?
Idaho

83. Mount Oratia is the highest point in the Kuskokwim Mountains of Alaska. These mountains begin west of Fairbanks and run southwest before ending at what bay, an inlet of the Bering Sea?
Bristol Bay

84. The International Peace Garden is shared by the Canadian province of Manitoba and what U.S. state?
North Dakota

85. What national monument can be found in the Crow Indian Reservation, Montana's largest reservation?
Little Bighorn Battlefield National Monument

86. Utah is home to one of the longest east/west mountain ranges in the United States. Name this mountain range.
Uinta Mountains

87. Ashley National Forest is located in northeastern Utah near the border with what other state?
Wyoming

88. The Rogue River is a popular destination for fishermen and whitewater rafters in the southwestern part of what state?
Oregon

89.   Utah's Wasatch-Cache national Forest has been merged with what
       other national forest to become operated as a combined national
       forest?
       **Uinta National Forest (Note: It is operated as the Uinta-
       Wasatch-Cache National Forest)**

90.   The Great Salt Lake, the largest natural lake west of the
       Mississippi River, is actually a remnant of a larger lake that
       existed during the Ice Age. Name this ancient lake.
       Lake Bonneville

91.   Mount Redoubt is the highest point in what Alaska mountain
       range that begins on the western shore of Cook Inlet?
       Aleutian Range

92.   Flathead Lake, the largest natural freshwater lake west of the
       Mississippi River, is in what state?
       Montana

93.   Name the second largest of all the freshwater lakes located west of
       the Mississippi River.
       Lake Tahoe

94.   In what state would you find the Talkeetna Mountains?
       Alaska

95.   Bird Island is located in the third largest freshwater lake west of
       the Mississippi River. Name this lake.
       Utah Lake

96.   The Bighorn Mountains and the Medicine Wheel, an ancient
       ceremonial site, are both located in what western state?
       Wyoming

97. The Thomas Condon Paleontology Center at John Day Fossil Beds National Monument attracts scientists to what state?
Oregon

98. The Powder River, which drains into the Yellowstone River in Montana, rises in what state?
Wyoming

99. A river running through southern Oregon and northern California once produced the third largest amount of salmon out of all U.S. river systems. Name this river that drains into the Pacific Ocean near Crescent City.
Klamath River

100. Mount Nebo is the highest point in what Utah mountain range?
Wasatch Range

101. The Salmon River is sometimes referred to as the "River of No Return" because of the difficulty of navigating upstream along its course. This river is a tributary of what larger river?
Snake River

102. Point Reyes National Seashore, well-known as a surfer's paradise, is in what state?
California

103. Malheur National Wildlife Refuge is home to a large lake and a wide variety of fauna. This refuge is located approximately 30 miles south of Burns in what state?
Oregon

104. Crater Lake is located in the caldera of what collapsed, ancient volcano?
Mount Mazama

105. The Sea Lion Cave System, America's largest sea cave system, is located about eleven miles north of Florence in what state?
Oregon

106. Balboa Park is located in what city in California?
San Diego

107. Waldo Lake is the second-deepest lake in what state?
Oregon

108. Umatilla National Forest encompasses most of the Blue Mountains, which span what two states?
Washington and Oregon

109. Eagle Peak is located in Yellowstone National Park in what state?
Wyoming

110. Name the 90-mile scenic highway that stretches from Carmel to San Simeon.
Big Sur Highway

111. Name the national park northwest of the Mojave Desert.
Death Valley National Park

112. Name the well-known stratovolcano located in the Cascade Range 60 miles north of Redding, California.
Mount Shasta

113. The town of Mexican Hat along the San Juan River is a base for exploring Monument Valley and Natural Bridges National Monument. This town is in what state?
Utah

114. What national marine sanctuary spans almost 1470 square miles and surrounds the islands of San Miguel, Santa Rosa, Santa Cruz, Anacapa and Santa Barbara?
Channel Islands National Marine Sanctuary

115. Washington's tri-cities region that has the cities of Richland, Pasco, and Kennewick is at the junction of the Snake River and what other tributary of the Columbia River?
Yakima River

116. The Papahanaumokuakea Marine National Monument extends from Kure Atoll, the most remote of the Northwestern Hawaiian Islands, to what small island at the southeastern end of the chain?
Nihao Island

117. The 125-foot tall Astoria column, built in 1926 near the mouth of the Columbia River, is decorated with historic scenes of exploration and settlement along the coast of what state in the Pacific Northwest?
Oregon

118. Name the National Marine Sanctuary, nicknamed "Serengeti of the Sea," that stretches from San Francisco to Cambria and is home to the country's largest kelp forests.
Monterey Bay National Marine Sanctuary

119. The Wah-Wah Mountains, the Confusion Range, and Sevier Lake are all located in what state?
Utah

120. Whidbey Island and Camano Island are located in what sound?
Puget Sound

121. The city of Chula Vista is home to an important U.S. Olympic Training Center. Chula Vista is in what state that borders Mexico?
California

122.   Telluride is a former mining town on the San Miguel River in what state whose southeastern corner is home to Comanche National Grassland?
Colorado

123.   What strait separates San Juan Islands from Vancouver Island?
Haro Strait

124.   The San Juan Islands are located in the Salish Sea, one of the world's largest and most biologically-rich inland seas. Puget Sound, the Strait of Juan de Fuca, and what other strait combine to form this inland sea?
Strait of Georgia

125.   What river flowing through North Cascades National Park is the center of the largest watershed emptying into Puget Sound?
Skagit River

126.   Vail, Aspen, and Telluride are well-known ski resorts in what state?
Colorado

127.   Inyo National Forest is shared by California and what bordering state?
Nevada

128.   Name the largest town in southwestern Colorado located south of San Juan National Forest in the Animas River Valley.
Durango

129.   Capitol Reef National Park is in what state?
Utah

130.   The Medicine Bow and Laramie Mountains are located on the border between Colorado and what state?
Wyoming

131. In 1859, gold was discovered along the Blue River in Breckenridge, the largest historic district in which Rocky Mountain state?
Colorado

132. Orcas Island, Lopez Island, and Shaw Island are part of what island group in Washington?
San Juan Islands

133. The Cape Arago Lighthouse, built on top of a historic Coos Indian village on Chief's Island, can be found in what Pacific state?
Oregon

134. Pikes Peak is in what mountain range west of Denver and Colorado Springs?
Front Range

135. Coeur d'Alene Indian Reservation is in the northern panhandle of what state bordering Washington?
Idaho

136. Ashland, a city known for its summer Shakespeare Festival, is located in what state that is home to the western endpoint of the Applegate Trail?
Oregon

137. Fort Clatsop was the winter encampment for the Corps of Discovery from December 1805 to March 1806. This present-day historic site is near what city at the mouth of the Columbia River?
Astoria

138. Black Canyon of the Gunnison National Park is in what state?
Colorado

139.   Crested Butte is an 1800s mining town and present-day National
        Historic District in what state?
        Colorado

140.   Pueblo, Colorado is located at the confluence of Fountain Creek
        and what other river?
        Arkansas River

141.   Fort Collins, Colorado is located on the Poudre River, a tributary
        of what larger river?
        South Platte River

142.   Which mountain is farther east – Pikes Peak or Mt. Elbert?
        Pikes Peak

143.   Place these mountain ranges in order according to their
        latitudes from north to south – Sacramento Mountains, Bighorn
        Mountains, Front Range.
        Bighorn Mountains, Front Range, and Sacramento Mountains

144.   The Milk River drains into the Missouri River in Montana just
        northeast of what lake?
        Fort Peck Lake

145.   The Clark Fork River drains into what lake in northwest
        Montana?
        Flathead Lake

146.   The Seward Peninsula, Alaska, is bordered by what sound to the
        south?
        Norton Sound

147.   Which Alaskan island lies farther south – St. Lawrence Island or
        Nunivak Island?
        Nunivak Island

148. Anchorage, Alaska, is located on Cook Inlet at the northern end of what peninsula?
Kenai Peninsula

149. Iliamna Lake is situated between Lake Clark National Park to the north and what national park to the south?
Katmai National Park

150. Name the largest city on Baranof Island, Alaska, part of the Alexander Archipelago.
Sitka

151. The Hetch Hetchy Aqueduct system supplies water to several major cities in what state?
California

152. Chula Vista, California, is southeast of what large city?
San Diego

153. Name the highest point in Great Basin National Park, southeast of Ely, Nevada.
Wheeler Peak

154. Mount Whitney is along the eastern edge of what national park?
Sequoia National Park

155. Moab, Utah, is southeast of what national park?
Arches National Park

156. Kiska Island, Alaska is part of what island group that is part of the Aleutian Chain?
Rat Islands

157. The city of Pocatello is east of American Falls Reservoir in what state?
Idaho

158.   "The Valley Isle" is to Maui as "the Friendly Isle" is to what?
       Molokai

159.   Name California's largest marine sanctuary.
       Monterey Bay National Marine Sanctuary

160.   The Truckee River drains into Pyramid Lake, Nevada and is the
       only outlet of what lake along the California-Nevada border?
       Lake Tahoe

161.   Aleutian World War II National Historic Area and Dutch Harbor
       are on Amaknak Island, located northeast of what larger island in
       the Fox Islands group?
       Unalaska Island

162.   Which Alaskan Island extends farther west – St. Matthew Island
       or Unimak Island?
       St. Matthew Island

163.   St. George, in the southwestern corner of Utah, is on the Virgin
       River, a tributary of what larger river?
       Colorado River

164.   The Palouse Region is a wheat-producing area in what state
       bordering Idaho and Oregon?
       Washington

165.   Which city is closer to the Trans-Alaska Pipeline – Fairbanks or
       Anchorage?
       Fairbanks

166.   The southernmost national park in California is divided into the
       Colorado Desert system and the Mojave Desert system. Name this
       national park.
       Joshua Tree National Park

167. The city of Modesto is about 24 miles south of Stockton in what large state?
California

168. Aberdeen is a city near Grays Harbor, an inlet of the Pacific Ocean in what state?
Washington

169. The city of Orem is east of what lake that shares its name with its home state?
Utah Lake

170. Mount Kawaikini is the highest point on what Hawaiian Island, home to Wailua, the only navigable river in the state?"
Kauai

171. Mount Shasta is the second highest peak in what mountain range?
Cascades

172. The McKenzie River drains into the Willamette River near what large city in Oregon?
Eugene

173. Lassen Volcanic National Park is in what state?
California

174. Dinosaur National Monument extends from Colorado into which bordering state?
Utah

175. Name the largest lake entirely in Nevada.
Pyramid Lake

176. The Centennial Mountains, which form part of the border between Idaho and Montana, are part of what larger sub-range of the Rocky Mountains?
Bitterroot Range

177. Lava Beds National Monument is an attraction along the western edge of Modoc National Forest in which state – Hawaii, California, or Alaska?
California

178. Mount Ka'ala is the highest peak on what Hawaiian Island, nicknamed "the Gathering Place"?
Oahu

179. Name the largest island in Washington's San Juan Island group.
Orcas Island

180. One of the largest inland lakes in North America is also the largest lake in Idaho. Name this lake.
Lake Pend Oreille

181. What mountain range runs along the eastern boundary of Colorado's Great Sand Dunes National Park?
Sangre de Cristo Mountains

182. Alaska's Matanuska River drains into what inlet?
Cook Inlet

183. The Kootenai National Forest is located in the northwest corner of Montana and the panhandle region of what state?
Idaho

184. The Bighorn River drains into what river in Montana?
Yellowstone River

185. What well-known town on the Seward Peninsula is the end-point of the Iditarod Sled Race?
Nome

186. The Colorado River Aqueduct runs from Lake Havasu, near Parker, Arizona to Lake Matthews, near Riverside in what state?
California

187. Kona is a well-known tourist destination on what Hawaiian Island?
Big Island (Hawaii)

188. Which of these islands in Washington's San Juan Island group extends farther south – Lopez Island or Orcas Island?
Lopez Island

189. Located near the southern tip of the Kenai Peninsula, what town is sometimes described as "where the land ends and the sea begins?"
Homer

190. Big Smoky Valley is situated between the Toquima Range and the Toiyabe Range in what state?
Nevada

191. Upper Klamath Lake and Lake Abet are in what state?
Oregon

192. The second largest island in the United States is separated from the mainland by the Shelikof Strait. Name this island.
Kodiak Island

193. Name Wyoming's largest natural lake.
Yellowstone Lake

194.   Place these lakes in order according to their longitudes from east
        to west – Flathead Lake, Fort Peck Lake, Lake Pend Oreille.
        Fort Peck Lake, Flathead Lake, and Lake Pend Oreille

195.   Name the largest lake west of the Mississippi River.
        Great Salt Lake

196.   The Porcupine River drains into what river in Alaska?
        Yukon River

197.   The Pailolo Channel separates Maui from what Hawaiian Island to
        the northwest?
        Molokai

198.   The Malaspina Glacier, the largest glacier in North America,
        drains into what gulf?
        Gulf of Alaska

199.   The Uncompahgre Plateau watershed includes the four major
        drainages of the Colorado River: the Uncompahgre River, San
        Miguel River, Dolores River, and what other river well known for
        its steep descent through the black canyons in the region?
        Gunnison River

200.   You are in Prudhoe Bay, Alaska. You decide to get into a
        helicopter tour offered by a local company. You are flying east and
        you see the Arctic National Wildlife Refuge to your right and
        you see a wide expanse of water bordering this refuge to its north.
        You look left and you realize you are looking at the Arctic Ocean.
        What outlying sea of the Arctic Ocean are you looking at along
        the northern shores of the Arctic National Wildlife Refuge?
        Beaufort Sea

CHAPTER 5

U.S. Southeast

1.   What state is home to the largest portion of the Blue Ridge
     Mountains?
     Virginia

2.   Which state does not border Alabama – Florida or Kentucky?
     Kentucky

3.   What state borders Missouri and Louisiana?
     Arkansas

4.   Which state does not border West Virginia – North Carolina or
     Ohio?
     North Carolina

5.   Which state borders more states – Kentucky or Georgia?
     Kentucky

6.   Which state borders the Atlantic Ocean – South Carolina or West
     Virginia?
     South Carolina

7.   What state borders North Carolina to the west?
     Tennessee

8.   Which southeastern state has a shorter coastline – Alabama or
     Mississippi?
     Alabama

9.   St. Petersburg, Florida is on what bay?
     Tampa Bay

10. Fort Pulaski National Monument can be found near Tybee Island
     in what state north of Florida?
     Georgia

11. Black Mountain is the highest point in what state that borders Virginia and Ohio?
Kentucky

12. The Chandeleur Islands belong to what state named after a famous French monarch?
Louisiana

13. J. Percy Priest Lake is located near Smyrna, a city in what state bordering Missouri and Georgia?
Tennessee

14. The Pee Dee River drains into the Atlantic Ocean in what state bordering Georgia and North Carolina?
South Carolina

15. Mount Vernon, home of President Washington, is in what state?
Virginia

16. Lower Suwannee National Wildlife Refuge is in what state that is home to the southernmost point in the contiguous United States?
Florida

17. The Croatan National Forest, traversed by the Neuse River, is in what state bordering Virginia and South Carolina?
North Carolina

18. White Sulphur Springs is a picturesque site in the Allegheny Mountains of what state whose highest point is Spruce Knob?
West Virginia

19. What state borders Arkansas and North Carolina?
Tennessee

20.   West Memphis is a city in the fertile, rice-growing region of the
       Mississippi Valley in what state?
       Arkansas

21.   What coastal state borders Georgia and Alabama?
       Florida

22.   What tributary of the Ohio River is formed by the Leviska
       Fork and Tug Fork Rivers along Kentucky's border with West
       Virginia?
       Big Sandy River

23.   Savannah's Beach is a popular tourist destination on Tybee Island,
       the easternmost point of what state?
       Georgia

24.   What strait connects the Gulf of Mexico with the Atlantic Ocean?
       Straits of Florida

25.   The Skidaway Institute of Oceanography is the headquarters of
       what National Marine Sanctuary located 16 miles east of Sapelo
       Island, Georgia?
       Gray's Reef National Marine Sanctuary

26.   What city became the colonial capital of Virginia in 1705?
       Williamsburg

27.   Chincoteague Island, well-known for its population of wild
       ponies, is a tourist attraction in what state?
       Virginia

28.   Shepherdstown and Charles Town, West Virginia are near what
       National Historic Park?
       Harpers Ferry National Historic Park

29. Name the largest subtropical wilderness in United States.
The Everglades

30. The easternmost point of the Trail of Tears is located at the roundup routes at Fort Lindsay. Fort Lindsay is in what state?
North Carolina

31. Name the largest river swamp in United States.
Atchafalaya Swamp

32. What state that is often called the Yellowhammer State has risen to number five in automobile production in the country?
Alabama

33. The Marshall Space Flight Center, one of NASA's largest installations that provide support to space missions, is located in what city north of the Tennessee River?
Huntsville

34. Russell Cave National Monument, home to prehistoric peoples for more than 10,000 years, is near Alabama's border with what state?
Tennessee

35. The Perdido River forms part of the border between Alabama and what state?
Florida

36. What swamp in the southeastern United States is considered to be the headwaters of the Suwannee and the St. Mary's Rivers?
Okefenokee Swamp

37. The Alabama Civil Rights Trail commemorates the 1965 historic march of demonstrators from Selma to what city?
Montgomery

38. Muscle Shoals Dam was built along the Tennessee River by what
     federally-owned corporation?
     Tennessee Valley Authority (TVA)

39. You can find tidal marshes along the Edisto River in what state?
     South Carolina

40. Dauphin Island, site of an important coastal research center, is
     part of a group of islands that encloses what sound?
     Mississippi Sound

41. Lewisburg, known for its Carnegie Hall cultural center, is in
     Greenbrier County in what state?
     West Virginia

42. Bald Knob is a mining town in West Virginia near the source of
     what river?
     Cheat River

43. What swamp spanning two states in the U.S. Southeast is named
     after a Native Indian word meaning "trembling earth"?
     Okefenokee Swamp

44. The Tallapoosa River begins in Georgia and flows southwest before
     joining the Coosa River near Montgomery to form what river?
     Alabama River

45. One of the largest freshwater complexes in the United States is a
     swamp sometimes known as the "river of grass." Name this region
     extending from Lake Okeechobee to the Straits of Florida.
     The Everglades

46. Cheaha Mountain is the highest point in what Alabama national
     forest that shares its name with a superspeedway?
     Talladega National Forest

47. In 1702, the French founded the first permanent European settlement in Alabama on an inlet of the Gulf of Mexico. Name this inlet.
Mobile Bay

48. The headquarters of what large retail corporation is located in Bentonville, Arkansas?
Wal-Mart

49. Hawksbill Crag or Whitaker Point overlooks what National Scenic River in Arkansas?
Buffalo National Scenic River

50. What park near Murfreesboro is the only diamond-producing area in the world that allows the public to keep what they find?
Crater of Diamonds State Park

51. Nine million gallons of water per hour flow from the world's largest spring, which is located in what state park in Arkansas?
Mammoth Spring State Park

52. The city of Texarkana, just southwest of Hope, the birthplace of President Bill Clinton, is located on the border of Arkansas and what other state?
Texas

53. What animal that is often called the "sea cow" is the state marine animal of Florida?
Manatee

54. Cape Sable is located at the southern end of what national park, home to the largest subtropical wilderness in the 48 contiguous states?
Everglades National Park

55. The oldest permanent European settlement on the continent was founded along the Atlantic Coast at what town on the Intracoastal Waterway north of Palm Coast?
St. Augustine

56. Juan Ponce de Leon, seeker of the fabled Fountain of Youth, claimed Florida in 1513, calling it "Pascua Florida" meaning Flowery Easter. For what European country did he claim Florida?
Spain

57. Name the highest point of Florida at only 345 feet above sea level, located in the panhandle region just south of the Alabama border.
Britton Hill

58. The Okefenokee National Wildlife Refuge, which harbors alligators, river otters, and bears in 700 square miles of untamed swamps, bogs, and marshes, spans the border between Georgia and what state?
Florida

59. What crop, also called "goobers," is related to alfalfa and beans and has been grown in Georgia since colonial times?
Peanuts

60. What charismatic African-American civil rights leader and recipient of the Nobel Peace Prize was born in Atlanta in 1929?
Martin Luther King Jr.

61. What mountain near Atlanta is famous for its enormous carving of three historic figures from the Confederate States of America – Stonewall Jackson, Robert E. Lee, and Jefferson Davis?
Stone Mountain

62.   James Oglethorpe founded a new colony in 1733 in what is now the oldest city in Georgia. Name this city, which shares its name with the river on which it is located.
        Savannah

63.   "Mountaineers Are Always Free" is the motto of which U.S. state?
        West Virginia

64.   Eastern Kentucky is rich in soft bituminous coal but burdened with environmental problems that often accompany the mining industry in what large mountain range?
        Appalachian Mountains

65.   Name the longest cave system in the world, located in west-central Kentucky.
        Mammoth Cave

66.   Churchill Downs, site of the famous Kentucky Derby, is located in what city?
        Louisville

67.   What region in central Kentucky, with a long, warm growing season and calcium-rich soils, yields excellent tobacco crops and prize-winning horses and provides an alternative source of income to the coal reserves in the east?
        Bluegrass Region

68.   Name the lake in the U.S. Southeast that is home to one of the longest causeways in the world at over 24 miles.
        Lake Pontchartrain

69.   What city is known as the City of the Dead because of its rows of tombs resembling city streets?
        New Orleans

70.   Many Cajuns in Louisiana are the descendants of people that once lived in the region of Acadia before being forced out by the British in the 1700s. What language do these Cajuns of Louisiana speak?
       French

71.   Name Louisiana's largest city.
       New Orleans

72.   Jackson, Mississippi is on what river?
       Pearl River

73.   The Marine Life Oceanarium, a major tourist attraction on the Gulf Coast that was almost destroyed by Hurricane Katrina in 2005, is located in what city west of Biloxi?
       Gulfport

74.   The Natchez Trace Parkway enters Tennessee from what bordering state?
       Alabama

75.   Hernando de Soto scouted Mississippi in 1540 and claimed it for what country before it was handed over to the French?
       Spain

76.   Name Mississippi's highest point.
       Woodall Mountain

77.   Name the North Carolina bay located between Cape Fear and Cape Lookout.
       Onslow Bay

78.   In 1903, the Wright Brothers achieved their first successful airplane flight near what town located in the Outer Banks east of Albemarle Sound?
       Kitty Hawk

79. Monitor National Marine Sanctuary, the nation's first national marine sanctuary, is located off the coast of what state?
North Carolina

80. Lake Gaston is on the border between North Carolina and what state?
Virginia

81. "Croatoan," a word carved on a tree on an island off the coast of North Carolina, was the only evidence of the vanished colony that became the first British settlement in the New World in 1587. Name this island.
Roanoke Island

82. Mt. Mitchell, the highest point east of the Mississippi River, is in what North Carolina national forest?
Pisgah National Forest

83. Name the city located where the Broad and Saluda Rivers merge to form the Congaree River.
Columbia

84. Name the South Carolina city that shares its name with a beach on Long Bay near the North Carolina border.
Myrtle Beach

85. Name the first and second largest lakes in South Carolina, located northwest of Francis Marion National Forest.
Lake Marion and Lake Moultrie

86. South Carolina was the first state to leave the union just months before the first shots of the Civil War were fired in 1861 on what fort?
Fort Sumter

87.   Reelfoot Lake is the largest natural lake in the northwestern part
        of what state near its borders with Kentucky and Missouri?
        Tennessee

88.   You can find wild turkeys in Francis Beidler Forest, a wildlife
        sanctuary and the world's largest virgin cypress-tupelo swamp
        forest, in what U.S. state?
        South Carolina

89.   Which state owns the Chandeleur Islands?
        Louisiana

90.   Pensacola, Florida is near the mouth of what river – Escambia
        River or Kissimmee River?
        Escambia River

91.   What national park attracts more visitors than any other U.S.
        national park?
        Great Smoky National Park

92.   Place these national parks in order according to the number of
        tourists they attract each year, from highest to lowest– Great
        Smoky Mountains National Park, Olympic National Park,
        Yellowstone National Park.
        **Great Smoky Mountains National Park, Yellowstone
        National Park, Olympic National Park**

93.   What river, a principal tributary of the Congaree River, provides
        water for Lake Murray in South Carolina?
        Saluda River

94.   The Intracoastal Waterway runs from Brownsville, Texas to St.
        Marks on Apalachee Bay in what state?
        Florida

95. Watts Bar Dam is one of nine Tennessee Valley Authority dams built to aid in navigation, flood control, and electrical power supply. This dam has saved many cities from flooding, including what large city located in the Cumberland Plateau near Tennessee's border with Georgia?
Chattanooga

96. Georgia's Ocmulgee and Oconee Rivers drain into what river that empties into the Atlantic Ocean near the Sea Islands?
Altamaha River

97. The city of Cary is situated west of what large North Carolina city?
Raleigh

98. Memphis, Tennessee is on what river?
Mississippi River

99. Land between the Lakes National Recreation Area, located between Kentucky Lake and Lake Barkley, is shared by Tennessee and what other state?
Kentucky

100. Pickwick Lake marks the northern terminus of what famous waterway?
Tennessee-Tombigbee Waterway

101. The final battle of the Revolutionary War was fought at what present-day city near Jamestown?
Yorktown

102. The Potomac, Rappahannock, and York Rivers all empty into what bay?
Chesapeake Bay

103.   George Washington National Forest and Jefferson National Forest
       span the border of Virginia and what other state?
       West Virginia

104.   Luray Caverns is in what national park?
       Shenandoah National Park

105.   The Monitor-Merrimac Bridge Tunnel is one of the longest in the
       world. It connects Newport News to what other city in Virginia?
       Suffolk

106.   The Chesapeake Bay Bridge Tunnel connects Kiptopeke State
       Park to the largest city in Virginia. Name this city.
       Virginia Beach

107.   Founded in 1751 by Robert Harper, Harper's Ferry was a
       departure point for pioneers heading west as well as the site of
       many Civil War battles. This town is located at the confluence of
       the Potomac and what other river?
       Shenandoah River

108.   Germany Valley, named after immigrants who moved there in the
       mid-1700s from North Carolina and Pennsylvania, is located in
       what national recreation area that contains West Virginia's highest
       point?
       Spruce Knob-Seneca Rocks National Recreation Area

109.   The Natchez Trace Parkway is a 444-mile road that runs through
       Alabama, Mississippi and what other state?
       Tennessee

110.   New River Gorge is considered to be the Grand Canyon of the
       East. What river in West Virginia is considered to be the Beast of
       the East?
       Gauley River

111. Cheat Mountain and Spruce Knob lie in what national forest in the Allegheny Mountains?
Monongahela National Forest

112. The Big Sandy and Tug Fork Rivers form the border between West Virginia and what other state?
Kentucky

113. What state produces more coal – Pennsylvania or Virginia?
Pennsylvania

114. The Alabama River joins what other river before draining into Mobile Bay?
Tombigbee River

115. The Black Warrior River, a tributary of the Tombigbee River, flows through the city of Tuscaloosa in what state?
Alabama

116. Crowley's Ridge is located east of Jonesboro in what southeastern state?
Arkansas

117. Pascagoula, north of Gulf Islands National Seashore, is in what southeastern state?
Mississippi

118. Bobcats are thriving on Kiawah Island, a resort community located southeast of Charleston in what southeastern state?
South Carolina

119. Daniel Boone National Forest is located near the Pine Mountain near the Virginia border in what state?
Kentucky

120.   Conecuh National Forest in located on the border between Florida
        and what southeastern state?
        Alabama

121.   Weirton, one of the few cities located at the junction of three
        states, is located in the northern panhandle of West Virginia.
        Name the two other states it borders.
        Ohio and Pennsylvania

122.   North Carolina's Roanoke River drains into what sound?
        Albemarle Sound

123.   The Saluda River in South Carolina drains into what river?
        Congaree River

124.   The Cape Fear River drains into the Atlantic Ocean near what city
        in North Carolina?
        Wilmington

125.   Boyles Island is on what river that drains into the Atlantic Ocean
        near Little St. Simons Island, part of the of the Sea Island chain in
        Georgia?
        Altamaha River

126.   The Suwannee River rises in Georgia and drains into the Gulf of
        Mexico in what state?
        Florida

127.   Russell Cave, near Bridgeport, was home to prehistoric people for
        more than 10,000 years. This monument is in what southeastern
        state?
        Alabama

128.   Name the large city in Tennessee near the Mississippi border.
        Memphis

129. Hattiesburg, Mississippi, is on the Leaf River, which drains into what larger river in the southeastern part of the state?
Pascagoula River

130. Melbourne and Port St. Lucie are coastal cities in what state?
Florida

131. The southernmost point of the Tennessee River is in what state?
Alabama

132. Walter F. George Reservoir is on what river that rises in the Blue Ridge Mountains and forms part of the border between Alabama and Georgia?
Chattahoochee River

133. The southernmost extent of Kentucky Lake is in what state?
Tennessee

134. The Nolin River and what other river flow through Mammoth Cave National Park?
Green River

135. Covington, Kentucky is just south of what large city?
Cincinnati

136. Which mountains in Arkansas make up part of Ozark National Forest – Ouachita Mountains or Boston Mountains?
Boston Mountains

137. The town of Corinth is west of Pickwick Lake in what state that borders Tennessee?
Mississippi

138. Cape Charles is a tourist town near the southern end of the Delmarva Peninsula in what state?
Virginia

139.   The Tennessee-Tombigbee Waterway links the Tennessee River in
        Mississippi to the Tombigbee River in what state?
        Alabama

140.   In 1792, what state that is home to parts of the Cumberland
        Plateau and the Ohio River became the first state west of the
        Appalachian Mountains to join the Union?
        Kentucky

141.   In 1864, General Sherman led the famous "March to the Sea" in
        which his troops marched from Atlanta to what historic coastal
        city?
        Savannah

142.   The 1862 Battle of Shiloh was fought in what state?
        Tennessee

143.   Meridian is an important city in what state that is home to Tupelo
        National Battlefield site?
        Mississippi

144.   Bon Secour National Wildlife Refuge is located on the Fort
        Morgan Peninsula west of the town of Gulf Shores in what state?
        Alabama

145.   Ocala National Forest borders Lake George in what state?
        Florida

146.   The Red River forms part of Arkansas's border with what state?
        Texas

147.   Owensboro, Kentucky is located near the Indiana border on what
        river?
        Ohio River

148. Ocmulgee National Monument is near the city of Macon in what state?
Georgia

149. Abraham Lincoln Birthplace National Historic Site is in which U.S. state?
Kentucky

150. Kisatchie National Forest is the largest national forest in what state that is home to the Mississippi River delta?
Louisiana

151. Manassas National Battlefield Park is in which U.S. state?
Virginia

152. The Ross Barnett Reservoir was created by damming the Pearl River in what state bordering Alabama and Tennessee?
Mississippi

153. Land Between the Lakes National Recreation Area is situated between two lakes that span Kentucky and Tennessee. Which of these lakes forms the eastern boundary of this recreation area?
Lake Barkley

154. Ocracoke Island borders Raleigh Bay in what state that shares Lake Gaston with Virginia?
North Carolina

155. Stonewall Jackson Lake in West Virginia was formed by damming the West Fork River. This river is a major tributary of what larger river that joins the Allegheny River in Pennsylvania?
Monongahela River

156. St. Helena Island is part of the Sea Islands in what state bordered by the Chattooga River to the northwest?
South Carolina

157.   In 1789, Virginia allowed its nine counties to apply for statehood
        and on June 1st 1792, these counties became the first U.S. state
        west of the Appalachian Mountains. Name this state.
        Kentucky

158.   Clingmans Dome, in the Great Smoky Mountains, is the highest
        point in what state?
        Tennessee

159.   The city of Mechanicsville is located just northeast of the historic
        capital of the Confederate States of America in what state?
        Virginia

160.   Woodall Mountain is to Mississippi as Mount Rogers is to what?
        Virginia

161.   The St. Mary's River forms part of the border between Georgia
        and what state?
        Florida

162.   The Licking River, a tributary of the Ohio River, separates the
        city of Newport, Kentucky from what city to the southwest?
        Covington

163.   Which river's mouth on the Chesapeake Bay is farthest north –
        the York River, the Rappahannock River, or the James River?
        Rappahannock River

164.   Lake Charles is a city on the Calcasieu River in what state
        bordering Texas and Mississippi?
        Louisiana

165.   Hampton Roads is a major cargo port in what state?
        Virginia

166. The Appalachian National Scenic Trail traverses which southeastern states?
Georgia, North Carolina, Tennessee, Virginia and West Virginia

167. Wheeling National Heritage Area on the Ohio River can be found in what state?
West Virginia

168. Fort Matanzas National Monument is near what historic coastal town in Florida?
St. Augustine

169. Which of these physical regions in Virginia is farthest east – Appalachian Plateau, Piedmont, or Blue Ridge Mountains?
Piedmont

170. The Chesapeake and Ohio Canal National Historic Park spans the District of Colombia, Maryland, and what state?
West Virginia

171. Charleston, West Virginia is to the Kanawha River as Richmond, Virginia is to what river?
James River

172. Jimmy Carter National Historic Site can be found in the town of Plains in what state?
Georgia

173. Gulf Islands National Seashore is a protected area in what two states?
Florida and Mississippi

174.   Mt. Mitchell is the highest point in the Black Mountains, part
        of what segment of the Appalachian Mountains extending
        southwestward from Pennsylvania to Georgia?
        Blue Ridge Mountains

175.   A large portion of the Cheat Mountain lies in Monongahela
        National Forest that has Spruce Knob as its highest peak. This is
        in which U.S. state?
        West Virginia

CHAPTER 6

U.S. Territories

1. What is the most populous island in the U.S. Caribbean territories?
Puerto Rico

2. What is the largest island in terms of area in the U.S. Pacific territories?
Guam

3. What is the most populous capital city in the U.S. Pacific territories?
Hagatna (Agana)

4. What is the most populous city in the U.S. Caribbean territories?
San Juan

5. What is the most populous island in the U.S. Pacific territories?
Guam

6. Which U.S. territory has a larger land area– US Virgin Islands or Northern Mariana Islands?
Northern Mariana Islands

7. Using the International Date Line as the reference, name the island that does not belong and explain why: Wake Island, Johnston Atoll, and Jarvis Island?
Wake Island because it is west of the International Date Line

8. Find the odd item out and explain why: Palmyra Atoll, Howland Island, and Jarvis Island?
Jarvis Island because it is south of the Equator

9. Lata Mountain, the highest point of American Samoa, is on what island in the Manu'a Island chain?
Tau

10. Name the island in the Caribbean Sea administered by the United States but used as a naval station by Haiti.
Navassa Island

11. Name the passage that separates Puerto Rico from the Dominican Republic.
Mona Passage

12. What term is used to describe the topography characterized by subterranean limestone caverns that are commonly found on islands in the Caribbean?
Karst (in Puerto Rico it is called the Northern Karst)

13. Name the largest island in the Atlantic Ocean that belongs to Puerto Rico, located just east of Puerto Rico.
Vieques Island

14. Name the city in Puerto Rico located west of Vega Baja that is known for its space observatory.
Arecibo

15. Name the city named after a wetland in Puerto Rico that lies south of the Caribbean National Forest and is called El Yunque by the natives.
Caguas

16. The city of Bayamon, Puerto Rico, lies to the southwest of what large city?
San Juan

17. Name the largest city on the Caribbean coast of Puerto Rico.
Ponce

18. Managaha Island sits in the blue green waters of a lagoon formed by a long reef along the western coast of the largest island in what U.S. territory known for its battles fought during World War II?
Northern Mariana Islands

19.   Buck Island National Wildlife Refuge is to St. Thomas as Buck
       Island Reef National Monument is to what?
       St Croix

20.   Crown Mountain, the highest point of the U.S. Virgin Islands, is
       on what island?
       St. Thomas

21.   What island is further south – St. Croix or St. John?
       St. Croix

22.   The brown tree snake is known to reduce bird and small mammal
       populations as well as cause power outages when it climbs power
       lines. This snake is famously associated with what U.S. Pacific
       territory that is home to War in the Pacific National Historic Park
       and Mt. Lamlam?
       Guam

23.   The city of San Jose is located on what island in the Pacific Ocean?
       Tinian

24.   Pago Pago, the capital of American Samoa, is located on what
       large island west of Aunuu?
       Tutuila

25.   The town of Dededo is located northeast of Apra Harbor on what
       island?
       Guam

26.   The village of Songsong is located on what island, the
       westernmost of the Northern Mariana Islands?
       Rota

27.   The National Park of American Samoa primarily spans Tutuila
       and the second largest American Samoan Island. Name this island.
       Tau

28.   Name the southernmost island of Northern Mariana Island chain
      excluding Guam.
      Rota

29.   Name the largest city on the western coast of Puerto Rico.
      Mayaguez

30.   The Virgin Islands were purchased by the United States from
      which country?
      Denmark

31.   Name the highest point in Puerto Rico located in the Cordillera
      Central.
      Cerro de Punta

32.   Agana Bay, Guam is separated from what bay to the northeast by
      the Oca Point escarpment?
      Tumon Bay

33.   Name the stout fortress, built in the 16th century that defended
      San Juan from attacks by sea for over three centuries, including an
      1895 attempt by Sir Francis Drake to loot its treasure.
      El Morro

34.   Many pharmaceutical factories can be found in the suburb of
      Manati on what island?
      Puerto Rico

35.   Microscopic organisms and algae luminesce to turn the ocean into
      a "sea of fire" at night in Puerto Rico's Phosphorescent Bay. This
      bay is located east of what lagoon?
      Laguna Cartagena

36.   Name the chief industry in American Samoa.
      Tuna canning

37. Name the group of people that are mixed descendants of both
     Spanish ancestors and the original inhabitants of Guam.
     Chamorro

38. Name the northernmost point on the island of Guam.
     Ritidian Point

39. What crop that is grown throughout the tropics has edible starchy
     root stocks – Taro or Potato?
     Taro

40. Name the small island in the territory of American Samoa, also
     called the Seventh Island, which lies 200 miles to the north of the
     islands of Savaii and Upolu.
     Swains Island

41. Name the air force base in Guam used by Japan and the United
     States that was also Amelia Earhart's final takeoff point before she
     disappeared mysteriously into the Pacific Ocean on July 2, 1937.
     Anderson Air Force Base

42. Pagan, Agrihan, and Anatahan are large volcanic islands in which
     U.S. territory?
     Northern Mariana Islands

43. Name the bay in eastern Guam located northeast of the town of Yona.
     Pago Bay

44. Name the island located between Kingman Reef and Kiritimati
     that is administered by the United States.
     Palmyra Atoll

45. Name the atoll owned by the United States that is located 940
     miles southwest of Hawaii.
     Johnston Atoll

46.   Islas de los Ladrones (Islands of the Thieves) is the name given by
       Spanish sailors in the early 16th century to what present day U.S.
       Commonwealth?
       Northern Mariana Islands

47.   Borinquen is the original Taino name of what U.S.
       Commonwealth?
       Puerto Rico

48.   Name U.S. Virgin Islands' largest ethnic group.
       Blacks

49.   Agrihan and Pagan are active volcanic islands in what U.S.
       territory?
       Northern Mariana Islands

50.   Cruz Bay is the main port on what island in the U.S. Virgin Island
       group?
       St. John

51.   What island located 13 miles off the west coast of Puerto Rico
       is managed as a National Wildlife Refuge by the U.S. Fish and
       Wildlife Service?
       Desecheo Island

52.   Name the southernmost island in the Marianas Island Chain.
       Guam

53.   The Maug Islands belong to what U.S. territory?
       Northern Mariana Islands

54.   Ofu, Olosega, and Tau Islands in American Samoa belong to what
       island group?
       Manua Islands

55. Culebra National Wildlife Refuge is in what U.S. territory?
Puerto Rico

56. Chamorro, Carolinian, and English are the official languages of what U.S. territory?
Northern Mariana Islands

57. Agat is a village on the Philippine Sea in what U.S. territory?
Guam

58. Frederiksted is to St. Croix as Cruz Bay is to what?
St. John

59. Carolina is the fourth largest city in what U.S. territory?
Puerto Rico

60. Tenleytown is the highest point of which U.S. federal district whose motto is Justicia Omnibus (Justice for All)?
District of Columbia

CHAPTER 7

U.S. Potluck

1.   The United States Constitution was signed in 1787 by the Constitutional Congress in what city?
      Philadelphia

2.   The Mormon Pioneer National Historic Trail begins in Nauvoo, a town near the Mississippi River in what state?
      Illinois

3.   Which state is the largest producer of milk?
      California

4.   Texas, Montana, California and what western state rank as the top four wool producers in the country?
      Wyoming

5.   Name the national marine sanctuary in the northwestern part of Lake Huron.
      Thunder Bay National Marine Sanctuary

6.   What mid-western state produces the most pork?
      Iowa

7.   Which is the only U.S. state that extends from the Great Lakes to the Atlantic Ocean?
      New York

8.   What mid-western state produces the most cheese?
      Wisconsin

9.   What state leads the nation in cotton production?
      Texas

10.   Wilmington, Delaware was founded in 1638 by settlers from what country?
      Sweden

11. Name the two states that lead in wheat production.
Kansas and North Dakota

12. What state leads in poultry production?
Georgia

13. Which state produces the most sheep?
Texas

14. The Star-Spangled Banner National Historic Trail runs through the District of Columbia and what two states?
Maryland and Virginia

15. What is the largest crop in terms of total production in the United States?
Corn

16. What crop is the second most planted field crop in United States?
Soybeans

17. What state accounts for almost 48 percent of rice production in the U.S.?
Arkansas

18. The Pony Express National Historic Trail stretches from San Francisco, California to St. Joseph in what midwestern state?
Missouri

19. The Ice Age National Scenic Trail stretches for over 1000 miles in what midwestern state?
Wisconsin

20. The United States is the leading producer and exporter of what crop that represents 50% of the world's oilseed production?
Soybeans

21.   What is the term for a structure used for storing grain and
        fermented animal feed – storage tank or silo?
        Silo

22.   What state capital city is near the mouth of the Severn River?
        Annapolis

23.   What two states share the only rounded boundary in the United
        States?
        Delaware and Pennsylvania

24.   The United States exports 10 percent of the world market of what
        crop grown mainly in the Arkansas Grand Prairie and the Gulf Coast?
        Rice

25.   Asbury Park features one of the best beaches in what mid-Atlantic
        state?
        New Jersey

26.   The El Camino Real de los Tejas National Historic Trail stretches
        from the Rio Grande to the Red River Valley and once extended
        to Mexico City. This trail spans what two states?
        Texas and Louisiana

27.   The Natchez Trace National Scenic Trail spans 450 miles in what
        state?
        Mississippi

28.   The Mall of the Americas is to Minnesota as the King of Prussia
        Mall is to what?
        Pennsylvania

29.   Jackson's Purchase is a historic region in the western part of what
        state in the Appalachian Highlands?
        Kentucky

30.   In June 2014, President Obama proposed expanding what Marine
       National Monument from almost 87,000 square miles to nearly
       782,000 square miles, which would make it the world's largest
       marine sanctuary?
       Pacific Remote Islands Marine National Monument

31.   The Nez Perce National Historic Trail begins at Wallowa Lake in
       Oregon and ends 40 miles from the Canadian border near the Bear
       Paw Mountains in what state?
       Montana

32.   Which state's population has a higher percentage people with
       Norwegian ancestry – Minnesota or Wisconsin?
       Minnesota

33.   The Maug Islands are part of what Marine National Monument in
       the Pacific that shares its name with a nearby trench?
       Marianas Trench Marine National Monument

34.   Which state's population has a higher percentage of people with
       Dutch ancestry – Pennsylvania or Michigan?
       Michigan

35.   Which state's population has a higher percentage of people with
       German ancestry – Pennsylvania or North Dakota?
       North Dakota

36.   Which state's population has a higher percentage of people with
       Irish ancestry – Massachusetts or New York?
       Massachusetts

37.   Which state's population has a higher percentage of people with
       Mexican ancestry –Texas or Arizona?
       Texas

38. In 1924, William Monroe Wright developed the Calumet Farm to breed and raise Standardbred horses in what southeastern state?
Kentucky

39. Flower Garden Banks National Marine Sanctuary is the only National Marine Sanctuary in what body of water that is sometimes referred to as the "Mediterranean of the Americas?"
Gulf of Mexico

40. The Fagatele Bay National Marine Sanctuary was recently renamed after what U.S. territory that owns Rose Atoll National Wildlife Refuge?
The National Marine Sanctuary of American Samoa

41. Which state's population has a higher percentage of people with Italian ancestry – Vermont or Rhode Island?
Rhode Island

42. The largest ancestry group in Wisconsin can trace its roots back to what European country?
Germany

43. What state's population has a higher percentage of Polish ancestry than any other state?
Wisconsin

44. What state's Native American population constitutes the largest percentage of its total population at 14.8%?
Alaska

45. The United States has controlled Guantanamo Bay, Cuba since the conclusion of what war in 1898?
Spanish-American War

46. Place these states in order in terms of their total Native American populations from highest to lowest – Oklahoma, California, New Mexico, and Arizona?
California, Oklahoma, Arizona, and New Mexico

47. What featured document of 1863 legally ended slavery in the United States?
Emancipation Proclamation

48. In 1565, the Spanish founded the first permanent European settlement in the United States. Name this settlement.
Saint Augustine

49. In 1585, the British built a settlement that later became known as the "Lost Colony" on what island in the Outer Banks of North Carolina?
Roanoke

50. Name the plateau that runs between the Appalachian Mountains and the Atlantic Coastal Plain.
Piedmont Plateau

51. Which mountain range has a higher elevation – Coast Range or Sierra Nevada?
Sierra Nevada

52. Which plateau has a higher elevation – Colorado Plateau or the Ozark Plateau?
Colorado Plateau

53. Which state has regions in a humid subtropical climate zone – Washington or Georgia?
Georgia

54. Which state is not in Tornado Alley – Oklahoma or Tennessee?
Tennessee

55. Which state experiences more hurricanes – Texas or California?
    Texas

56. Which state has a higher gross domestic product – California or Texas?
    California

57. What southeastern state, along with the Tornado Alley Region, experiences a disproportionately high frequency of tornadoes?
    Florida

58. The longest of America's eleven congressionally designated national scenic trails links seven states — New York, Pennsylvania, Ohio, Michigan, Wisconsin, Minnesota, and North Dakota. Name this 4,600-mile-long trail.
    North Country National Scenic Trail

59. Name the region made up of southern and western states that are experiencing major migration and rapid economic growth.
    Sun Belt

60. Name the simplified or modern form of a language that is used for communication between two groups and developed from a pidgin.
    Creole

61. Name the major climate type, abbreviated "H" in the Koppen classification system that is associated with high mountains and elevations affecting temperature and precipitation.
    Highland climate

62. What is the term for total value of all goods and services produced in a country in a year?
    Gross Domestic Product (GDP)

63. What is the major climate type found on the West Coast of the U.S. in areas such as Oregon and Washington?
Marine West Coast

64. What is the term for the major climate type, characterized by warm summers and mild winters that can be found at lower latitudes than regions with Marine West Coast climate?
Mediterranean

65. What is the term for the irrigation system in United States involving a piped water source that rotates around as its middle, resulting in circular field patterns – Center pivot or Drip irrigation?
Center pivot

66. What is the term for an embankment, usually constructed out of earth or concrete that is designed to prevent a river from overflowing?
Levee or Dyke

67. What is the longest river system in the United States?
Mississippi-Missouri River system

68. Lindbergh Field International Airport is to San Diego, California as Louis Armstrong International Airport is to what?
New Orleans

69. Sky Harbor International Airport is to Phoenix, Arizona as Logan International Airport is to what?
Boston

70. John F. Kennedy International Airport is to New York City as George Bush Intercontinental Airport is to what?
Houston

71.   What is the lowest point in the United States?
        Death Valley

72.   The lowest temperature in the United States was recorded at
        Prospect Creek in what state?
        Alaska

73.   The majority of the population of the United States is of what
        ethnicity?
        White

74.   George Washington appointed Pierre L'Enfant to design the city
        of Washington D.C. at the junction of the Potomac River and
        what river?
        Anacostia River

75.   Name the body of water in Washington D.C. bounded by Kutz
        Bridge on the north and Inlet Bridge on the south.
        Tidal Basin

76.   Name the channel that is located just north of the Theodore
        Roosevelt Memorial Bridge in Washington D.C.
        Georgetown Channel

77.   What state leads in steel production – Oregon or Pennsylvania?
        Pennsylvania

78.   Which U.S. state has more broadleaf forest vegetation – Illinois or
        Colorado?
        Illinois

79.   Which U.S. state has more needle leaf forest vegetation – Nevada
        or North Dakota?
        Nevada

80. Which U.S. state can have more mixed forest vegetation –
Wisconsin or Tennessee?
Wisconsin

81. Which U.S. state can have more grassland vegetation – Nebraska
or Washington?
Nebraska

82. Which U.S. state has more needle leaf vegetation – Nebraska or
Minnesota?
Minnesota

83. Which U.S. state has more desert vegetation – Texas or Colorado?
Texas

84. Which U.S. state experiences warm summer continental climate –
Pennsylvania or Indiana?
Pennsylvania

85. Which U.S. state experiences more humid subtropical climate –
Iowa or Kansas?
Kansas

86. Subarctic climate is more common in which U.S. state –
California or Alaska?
Alaska

87. Which U.S. state has a more tropical wet and dry climate –
Florida or Hawaii?
Hawaii

88. Which U.S. state has a more humid subtropical climate – New
Jersey or Rhode Island?
New Jersey

89.   Which U.S. state has a lower potential for biomass – Missouri or
        Wyoming?
        Wyoming

90.   Which U.S. state has a higher solar electric capacity per capita –
        Arizona or New Mexico?
        Arizona

91.   Which state has a higher biomass potential – Minnesota,
        Michigan or New York?
        Minnesota

92.   Which mid-western city, nicknamed the "Mile High City" is
        Nairobi, Kenya's sister city?
        Denver

93.   Which state is located entirely within the Central Time
        Zone – North Dakota, South Dakota, Minnesota or
        Kansas?
        Minnesota

94.   Name the odd item out in terms of time zones: Florida, Georgia,
        and South Carolina
        **Florida as it is partially in Central Time Zone while others
        are in the Eastern Time Zone**

95.   Name the odd item out in terms of time zones: Nevada, New
        Mexico, Colorado
        Nevada as it is in Western Time Zone

96.   What state was originally part of the Oregon Country – Idaho,
        Nevada, or California?
        Idaho

97.   Which U.S. state was acquired from Mexico as part of the
       Gadsden Purchase in 1853 - Arizona, Kansas, or Arkansas?
       Arizona

98.   Which state has a higher population density – Tennessee or Montana?
       Tennessee

99.   Which state has a higher population density – Iowa or New
       Hampshire?
       New Hampshire

100.   In what state is a larger percentage of the population of African
       American decent - Alabama or Nevada?
       Alabama

101.   In what state does a larger percentage of the population consist of
       Native Americans – Nevada or Oregon?
       Nevada

102.   In what state is a larger percentage of the population of Latino
       decent – North Carolina or Ohio?
       North Carolina

103.   In what state is a larger percentage of the population of Asian
       descent – Washington or New York?
       Washington

104.   Which state has a higher population density – Montana or
       Missouri?
       Missouri

105.   Which U.S. state is not among the Top Ten in Farm Products by
       net farm income – Nebraska, Wyoming, or Illinois?
       Wyoming

106.   What state has more fisheries – Maine, Louisiana, or Alaska?
        Alaska

107.   What state is among the top ten in the production of minerals –
        Minnesota, Oklahoma, or Hawaii?
        Minnesota

108.   What state leads in the production of crabs, pollock, and salmon
        in the country?
        Alaska

109.   What state is not among the top five in the production of salmon
        – Oregon, Maine, or Florida?
        Florida

110.   What state is a leading turkey producer – Minnesota, California,
        or New Jersey?
        Minnesota

111.   What state is a leading corn producer – Illinois or Louisiana?
        Illinois

112.   What state is a leading cattle producer – Kansas or Arizona?
        Kansas

113.   In what two states could you find "tropical wet" and "tropical wet
        and dry" climate zones?
        Florida and Hawaii

114.   Most of Texas is in which climate zone – Humid subtropical or
        Arid?
        Humid subtropical

115.   Which part of United States has experienced the most rapid
        population growth – Sunbelt or the East Coast?
        Sunbelt

116.   The Baby Boomer generation refers to the portion of the
        population that was born immediately after what war – The
        Vietnam War or The World War II?
        The World War II

117.   Most of the population of the United States is of what descent –
        Asian, Latin American or European?
        European

118.   Which state has a higher Hispanic population by percentage –
        Florida or Oregon?
        Florida

119.   Where would you find a larger population of Asian descent –
        Southwest or Northeast?
        Northeast

120.   Asheville, North Carolina provides an access point to Pisgah
        National Forest, Nantahala National Forest, and what national
        park along the Tennessee border?
        Great Smoky Mountains National Park

121.   The Blue Ridge Mountains extend southwestward from Carlisle,
        Pennsylvania to Mt. Oglethorpe in what state?
        Georgia

122.   Name all the states crossed by the Blue Ridge Mountains.
        **Pennsylvania, Virginia, Maryland, North Carolina, South
        Carolina, and Georgia**

123. Name the most active seismic region east of the Rocky Mountains that extends for about 125 miles through Arkansas, Missouri, Tennessee, and Kentucky.
New Madrid Seismic Zone

124. Which region has the highest density of active faults of any urban area in the United States – the San Francisco Bay Area or the Anchorage region?
San Francisco Bay Area

125. Motion between three plates off the coast of the Pacific Northwest causes frequent earthquakes. Name these three plates.
North American, Pacific, and Juan de Fuca plates

126. The 1893 Sea Islands Hurricane is considered to be one of the deadliest hurricanes to hit the United States. This hurricane made landfall along the coast of what state?
Georgia

127. Which state, while being the largest producer of macadamia nuts in the country, is also a major producer of coffee?
Hawaii

128. In 2014, a toxic algae boom caused major ecological problems for cities located on what Great Lake that has the southernmost point on Canada's mainland?
Lake Erie

129. The Bristol Motor Speedway, located in the town of Bristol, is one of the nation's most popular NASCAR venues. This historic town, also considered to be the birthplace of country music, is near what state's border with Virginia?
Tennessee

130. Which city was part of New Spain – Santa Fe, New Mexico or
      Denver, Colorado?
      Santa Fe

131. In 1638, Swedish and Finnish colonists set up a timber fort in an
      area within Fort Christina National Historic Landmark in what
      state?
      Delaware

132. By 1750 there were thirteen British colonies along the
      Atlantic coast of North America. Name the southernmost and
      northernmost of these colonies.
      Georgia-Southernmost, Massachusetts-Northernmost

133. In 1750, what was the most populous of the thirteen original
      colonies?
      Virginia

134. Early American settlements consisting of people from
      which country were mainly trading posts instead of farming
      communities – Great Britain or Sweden?
      Sweden

135. Watkins Glen, site of a major Formula 1 race track until 1980, is
      at the southern tip of Seneca Lake in what state?
      New York

136. Canaan Valley National Wildlife Refuge in the Allegheny
      Mountains is a large wetland area in what state?
      West Virginia

137. Ford Island, site of a major bombing during World War II, is in
      what state?
      Hawaii

138.   What was the name given to the 150,000-square-mile area
        spanning the Oklahoma and Texas panhandles and sections of
        Kansas, Colorado, and New Mexico that was decimated by a
        destructive mix of poor rainfall, light soil, and high winds in the
        1930s?
        Dust Bowl

139.   The Rappahannock River is one of the major sources of water flow
        into the largest estuary system in the contiguous United States.
        Name this system.
        Chesapeake Bay

140.   The sixth-largest inland body of water in United States can be
        found in the Northeast near Canada. Name this body of water.
        Lake Champlain

141.   Apalachicola Bay is to Florida as Tillamook Bay is to what?
        Oregon

142.   The northern isthmus of what peninsula is traversed by the
        Chesapeake and Delaware Canal?
        Delmarva Peninsula

143.   Name the largest island in Chesapeake Bay.
        Kent Island

144.   Name the only Mid-Atlantic state that does not border the
        Atlantic Ocean.
        Pennsylvania

145.   What state is a leading producer of sulfur and salt - Louisiana or
        Missouri?
        Louisiana

BIBLIOGRAPHY

Bockenhauer, Mark H. *Our Fifty States*. Washington, D.C: National
     Geographic, 2004.

Britannica Online Encyclopaedia. http://www.britannica.com/.

National Geographic Society. *National Geographic Kids United States Atlas*.
     Washington, DC: National Geographic Society, 2012.

Wikipedia: The Free Encyclopedia. http://www.wikipedia.org/. Accessed
     Jan 2014–Dec 2014.

U.S. Fish and Worldlife Service. http://www.fws.gov/. Accessed Jan
     2014–Dec 2014.

American Society of Civil Engineers. http://www.asce.org/. Accessed Jan
     2014–Dec 2014.

National Park Service. http://www.nps.gov/. Accessed Jan 2014–Dec
     2014.

Missouri Department of Natural Resources. http://www.dnr.mo.gov/.
     Accessed Jan 2014–Dec 2014.

U.S. Geological Survey. http://www.usgs.gov/. Accessed Jan 2014–Dec
     2014.

National Agricultural Statistics Service. http://www.nass.usda.gov/. Accessed Jan 2014–Dec 2014.

Library of Virginia. http://www.lva.virginia.gov/public/kentucky/. Accessed Jan 2015-Feb 2015.

Alberta Agricultural and Rural Development. http://www1.agric.gov.ab.ca/$department/deptdocs.nsf/all/sis5219/. Accessed Jan 2014–Dec 2014.

History Channel. http://www.history.com/topics/dust-bowl. Accessed Jan 2014–Dec 2014.

United States Environmental Protection Agency. http://www.epa.gov/. Accessed Jan 2014–Dec 2014.

National Oceanic and Atmospheric Administration. http://www.noaa.gov/. Accessed Jan 2014–Dec 2014.

U.S. Department of Agriculture. http://www.fs.usda.gov/. Accessed Jan 2014–Dec 2014.

Solar Energy Industries Association. http://www.seia.org/.Accessed Jan 2015-Feb 2015.

ABOUT THE AUTHOR

Ram Iyer lives in the Kansas City area and is self-employed. Although he has spent most of his career in the engineering field, his interests extend into the physical sciences, earth sciences, geography, history, world cultures, sports, and political science.

He wrote his first guide, *Geography Bee Demystified*, mainly to help students prepare for the National Geographic Bee- at both the State and the National levels. Based on reader responses, he felt there was a need for a second guide that would help budding geographers ease into the rigors of the competition. Accordingly, *Geography Bee Simplified*, a prequel to his first guide, came to fruition. He observed that the best students of geography have found themselves lacking when it came to challenging questions in U.S. geography in their School and State Geography Bees. *Geography Bee Declassified – U.S. Files* is an attempt to address that concern.

Ram and his family live in Olathe, Kansas.

ABOUT THE EDITOR

Gentry Clark became fascinated by maps even before entering kindergarten. When he was five years old, one of his favorite pastimes was having his mom drive him around his hometown of Austin, Texas, finding previously unknown streets, following along on his own personal key map, and directing her along mysterious and unusual paths. When his mom gave him his first geography book, he was hooked.

At nine, Gentry watched his first Geography Bee on PBS, and he talked his family into organizing the first annual Geography Bee for homeschoolers in the Austin area. For the next five years, Gentry lived and breathed geography. He pored over every video of past Bees that he could get his hands on, got lost for huge chunks of time in the world of tracing maps from the *National Geographic Atlas of the World,* and spent hundreds of hours quizzing with his dad, using the thousands of maps his father created for studying.

Gentry qualified for the Texas State Geographic Bee four years and ranked in two of those. During those four years, he competed against three eventual winners of the National Geography Bee. During his geography years, Gentry pursued his interests in chess, martial arts, soccer, and science. In middle school, he began his journey in science, competing in both Science Olympiad and Science Bowl as team captain, and becoming the first president of the High School Science Team. He plans to major in a STEM field in college.

The one rival for his dedication to science is his passion for music. He began studying guitar and music theory when he was twelve, and has traveled and performed with his music school's national demo team. He is now combining his fascination with engineering with his love of music and is building his own custom guitar from scratch. If he could figure out a way to make that guitar do dual duty as a combat robot, he'd be in heaven.

While Gentry finished just short of his goal to win the National Geography Bee, his years of study gave him more than any trophy could: a lifelong fascination with the earth and a knowledge of the workings of the world that has made him a true global citizen. He has continued his interest in geography by organizing a geography study group for middle schoolers and coordinating the annual National Geography Bee for homeschoolers in the Austin area.

Gentry owes a huge debt of gratitude to Ram Iyer for this opportunity to edit this guide. His journey through high school and on to college would have been a very different and less rewarding one without his association with Ram. Gentry is proud to count Ram and his family as lifelong friends.